OM *for the* HOME

A Holistic Approach to Interior Design for Your Overall Well-being, Body, Mind and Spirit

High Star Publishing

Carrie Leskowitz: carrie@carrieleskowitzinteriors.com

ISBN: 978-0-578-89393-8 (print)
ISBN: 978-0-578-90728-4 (ebook)

Ordering Information:
Special discounts are available on quantity purchases by corporations, associations, and others. For details, contact carrie@carieleskowitzinteriors.com

OM *for the* HOME

A Holistic Approach to Interior Design for Your Overall Well-being, Body, Mind and Spirit

CARRIE LESKOWITZ

FOREWORD BY CLODAGH

TABLE OF CONTENTS

Jason and Dylan, you're the reason my heart beats. Follow your intuition and look for synchronicities in life.

Steven, if home is the feeling of safely and calm, where you are is home. None of this means anything without you. Thank you for inspiring me every day to be and do better!

FOREWORD

By Clodagh

THE PRIMEVAL SOUND OF CREATION: A MANTRA.

Carrie has clarified brilliantly the myth that an interior designer is not just an interior designer, but has to act and talk like a life coach. To make sure she was doing things right, she actually became a life coach, earning a degree and adding this wisdom to her perception about what a home—or indeed an office—is all about.

Since I was a teenager, I have been moaning about the education I got at boarding school that I have never used since, including differential calculus and the names of global capital cities—never an insider's view of the cultures in other countries, which would have been more helpful. Also, endless sports like hockey and tennis, where I gained only one piece of knowledge about myself that helped: I am not competitive, I just want to win.

Why was I not taught how to live, converse, create my own environment, manage a living space, make love, negotiate, cook, and budget with a manual to consult as I wove my life and designed? Why was I not taught to take care of my body and soul?

You cannot buy kitchen appliances without an accompanying manual. Yet we, with our bodies and souls, are sent out into the world without anything to consult except for our brain. As I say, "Life is all practice and then you die." Carrie has practiced for us.

Carrie, with her brilliant professional combination of interior designer and life coach, has created a manual for living that is accessible and understandable on every page. In 13 chapters, she has summarized—with touching and revealing real-life examples—how to make positive tectonic shifts in your daily life; how to step back and think before you step forward. She teaches her clients like a travel guide would, bringing them places where they want to go to and then challenging them to go further to discover new places in their souls and to expose dreams they never imagine discovering. In Imprinted past (Chapter Three) she describes how memories can be triggered by an object or a color to release that inner private video that we all carry within. She teaches us to examine ourselves and challenge ourselves.

She teaches us that design goes beyond the physical, and good design, together with Feng Shui and healing, makes the invisible tangible.

Carrie understands the tenets of working with the elements and the use of color, light, sound, and fragrance to trigger the senses and produce positive emotions to support well-being.

And she knows too many of us are suffocated by stuff. In Chapter Four, Carrie shows how clutter brings stagnation, and even paralysis, which hoarders can experience. She shows us that a home should have a place for everything, with everything in its place. Le Corbusier qualified a house as "a machine for living," and this doesn't stop with the walls and windows and doors, this applies to every facet of the interior. Like any other machine, a house needs to be cleaned and fueled and work.

Good design must work.

Carrie's book is the best gift you can give to YOURSELF AND TO PEOPLE OF ALL AGES as a guide to move freely through space and time without the excess baggage of emotional and visual clutter to hamper their lives. She shows us that unfettered living is possible.

The intensive research which fueled this book is stunning.

Thank you, Carrie, for this life manual. It will help to make the world a better place. It will have a special place on my bookshelf!

Clodagh

One of the top designers in the world and a globally in-demand inspirational speaker, Clodagh is recognized as a leader in sustainable design. She is an environmentalist, philanthropist and inducted into the Interior Design Hall of Fame. Her projects appeal to all the senses, enriched with unmistakable warmth and beauty though authentic materials and the use of natural elements. Clodagh's newest book, Clodagh: Life-Enhancing Design was published 2018. Her previous titles include Your Home, Your Sanctuary and Total Design, now in its third printing.

1

OM SWEET hOMe

Home Is a Metaphor for Our Soul

YOUR HOME IS WITHIN YOU AND OUTSIDE OF YOU. Whether we are talking about the human body or your living space, they are both vessels for your soul. Your home is so much more than an address. Home is experiential. It should capture your attention, integrate all your senses and allow you to explore what's possible. It should be your sacred, safe space to land; it is your spiritual compass, pointing the direction to your north star. There is great power in making your home into a hOMe.

Think of your home as a giant living vision board, helping you aspire to and manifest goals. It is a foundation for your identity, telling all who enter how you see yourself and what you value. Your home is an anchor in the storm, safely keeping you moored to who you are in a way that nothing else can. You want to intentionally create environments that help you thrive physically, emotionally, and spiritually because there is a deep synergy between our inner state and our outer state. Consciously creating a home that supports you in mind, body, and spirit—and that mirrors your authenticity—is an act of self-care of the highest order. Your home is a state of mind as well as a self-portrait. Others look at your home and make assumptions based on the picture you paint.

When I talk about om for the home, I am talking about it in terms of energy, an energy whose balance requires that you need to be very mindful and thoughtful in your effort to feel your best in your hOMe. For me, that starts with a stillness that isn't always easy to achieve.

In yoga class one day, I found it very hard to sit still and quiet my mind, especially in what I consider the uncomfortable lotus position. I focused on simple in and out breathing as thoughts would come and go. I tried to let go of resistance, observing whatever discomfort might come up physically or emotionally, all the while thinking, Oh, sweet Shavasana, you cannot come soon enough!

I reminded myself that they call yoga "a practice" for a reason and that it is helping me to connect my mind, body, and spirit. I engage everything I have in order to alter the energy I exude, quiet my mind, center my being, raise my vibration, and let go of what I cannot control. Yoga's benefits are near limitless. I wanted more of that! My practice is a work in progress. I am a work in process.

And so is the physical space we live in.

We breathe, we grow, we dream, we love, we suffer, we rejoice within the walls of our dwelling. Those walls better be pretty stable to support the "heavy lifting" necessary to make us feel safe, sound, and seen. To be mindful of the importance of home from a philosophical standpoint is to be aware that your inner self and outer self are intertwined—that everything is intertwined. You need to pay attention to what makes you feel most at home. Whatever makes you feel grounded, secure, at peace: go there. When you step over the threshold, you want—always—to find yourself in that place you consider home. When you lose your way, home reminds you of where you've been and where you're going.

I have been an interior designer for 20 plus years and became a life coach a few years ago. Combining the two careers has helped me create a language between myself and my clients. I understand when working with clients that there's a deep connection between their home and what goes on in their lives—their relationship to others and to themselves.

There are messages in the mess. I can identify them. So, my clients are not just getting a transformation of their homes when they work with me, but a transformative experience to better their lives.

My Home Lacks a Strong Identity

My client Kathy and I created a vacation home together. All that Kathy aspired to be was a good mother. She knew even as a young girl that she wanted a husband, children, a home. That would be her life's work. I've known women like this my whole life. They are 100 percent invested in the family, and that's great—until it isn't.

Kathy's vacation home was a place by the beach where she and her family could escape the city. The goal was to create "a home away from home" that hopefully her extended family and, eventually, her grandchildren would enjoy for years to come.

She was very clear about the look she was going for: very neutral, extremely neutral, unapologetically neutral. I love a neutral environment as much as the next person, as long as it incorporates a lot of texture. This is because, when designing a monochromatic space, the interest needs to come from that texture—otherwise, you're faced with one big, beige space lacking in anything that gives it character. Kathy was on board.

The foundational furnishings (sofas, beds, custom ottoman, custom carpets, tables, and chairs) were all in shades of beige and taupe. We created interest through the weave of the fabrics; the coarseness of the natural fiber rugs; the hand of the organic, natural textiles; the slub of the silk; the fuzzy wool pillows and a chunky knit throw. Excellent. It was shaping up and looking beautiful.

Once the foundation was complete, it was time for the icing on the cake: the art and accessories. This is always the fun stuff. This is where you put your stamp on the design. This is where you say who you are. As your home tells the story of you, I wondered—what story we should tell of Kathy?

"Do you want to create a quintessential beach vibe?" I asked. "There's a beautiful flowering tree outside the window—let's bring the outside in with shades of pinks and greens, perhaps. Or maybe warm tones inspired by the sunshine—orange and ochre make sense."

I brought in so many lovely things, color combination after color combination. But Kathy was paralyzed, unable to make a decision. Nothing seemed to appeal to her. She said she was afraid of making a mistake. She was stuck.

Because I had gotten to know her, as I do all my design clients, I knew full well what was stopping Kathy in her tracks. Her youngest child was set to leave for college and this had sent her into a tailspin. Empty-nest syndrome is real and it can be terrifying. Kathy's fear kept her from moving forward and it manifested in the decor of her home. How could she tell the story of "Kathy" if she didn't know what her story was? Who was she authentically? She had only identified as a child, then a wife, then a mother. This new transition was, in a word, traumatic. Who would she be? What was to be her role moving forward—her new normal?

Because it was important for her to "get it right," her fear of making a mistake was commendable—she was astute enough to know what she didn't know. The correlation between accessorizing the family home and the loss of identity within Kathy was remarkable. However, I thought of it as an opportunity for her to learn something about herself. Start bringing a few things in slowly, live with them a bit and assess along the way. After all, every discovery process involves trial and error. When you have to do hard things, you must begin before you are ready—because (often times) you may never be ready.

Your home is a reflection of your soul, telling others who you are, what you value, where you've been and where you're going. In order to accomplish this, you need to have a clear picture of those things.

In this way, examining your home environment is an amazing opportunity for self exploration and reinvention. A foundation, minimally finished, without framing, is just raw space; however, it also provides an opportunity to "build-out" or "reframe" your identity if need be. It allows you to get in touch with your authentic self, your likes, dislikes, passions, gifts, and sense of curiosity. And, yes, your shadow side too. All must be considered and accepted to feel truly whole. You will not find your authentic self in the skills you have acquired to please other people, or even in those skills that you have become really adept at if they do not speak to a higher passion and a sense of purpose.

When I pointed out my observation to Kathy, she was struck by it all. She might not have been ready to embrace the idea, but it did give her food for thought.

Since, as a designer, my job is to help my clients achieve a beautiful, functional, sacred space, I achieved that goal to some degree. I'd be lying if I said it didn't kill me to walk away from that job without all the "pretty" in place. I could educate, but I would not push. As a life coach, I am obligated to meet people where they are. I felt a little disappointed that my client was not open to that kind of self-discovery yet, so totally beige it stayed. Oh, the places we could go. We all do things in our own time. I gave Kathy some tips to set her on a path of self-discovery if she chose to do so in the future and wished her well.

As with Kathy, discovering your authentic self requires great introspection. You must be willing to show up, be vulnerable, and let go of expectations and fear. Just observe and be open to the process. Recognize that it takes time to develop a sense of how to reflect yourself authentically in your home precisely because it can feel uncomfortable. Growth can feel uncomfortable.

Otherwise, you will stay exactly where you are now. You may need time to reflect and resolve old traumas or experiences and beliefs as you explore, question, probe, examine.

Start by responding to these fundamental questions:

"What do I stand for?"
"What are my values?"
"What, or who inspires me?"
"Who would I be without definitions others have of me?"
"What brings me joy?"
"What brings me sadness?"
"What depletes my energy; what elevates it?"
"What is my soul seeking?"
"What am I most curious about?"
"What do I find deeply meaningful?"
"What do I believe my purpose is?"

Once you have an answer to the questions above, write a personal mission statement. A few sentences summarizing what information you gleaned from above. Having a personal mission statement is important because it motivates you and keeps you moving toward a more actualized identity. This will help to keep you focused on who you believe yourself to be, what is important to you, and how you want to frame your life moving forward. Then, decorate accordingly. Your home's interiors will reflect those values and characteristics intentionally and authentically! Always reassessing along the way because as we change and grow, so should our environment.

Answering these questions will help bring to light what fulfills you, what you value, and what is directly tied to your level of happiness. The more authentic you are, the better you feel in your own skin and within the walls of your home, and the happier you will be.

It is a solitary journey—one that forces you to go within. As you proceed, show yourself loving kindness. There's no right or wrong. There's only you.

Because life is fluid and change is certain, you must adapt to its twists and turns. Your identity is constantly evolving. This can be incredibly hard for those who have spent the majority of their energy focused on other people's needs, being a people pleaser, or even being a narcissist.

The journey begins with the need to develop awareness. When you are really in touch with yourself and know yourself innately, you will notice when something feels "off" and will be much better equipped to course correct. The answers come bit-by-bit, step-by-step. You will know you are walking the proper path because you will listen to that inner voice that tells you to keep going—This feels right. This makes sense for me.

Remember that self-discovery or rediscovery is the greatest gift you can give yourself. It is the deepest act of self-love. You are surrendering to you. You are meant to emerge as your highest self, as spiritual podcaster and writer Sahara Rose says:[1]

"In not knowing who she really was, my client reminded me of the film, *Runaway Bride (1999),* where the character of Maggie had almost wed many times, but each time she would leave the new fiancé at the altar.[2] When Ike, a handsome reporter, was sent to write her story, they fell in love, and he asked her to marry him. You want to believe this time it will be different, but as Maggie walks down the aisle toward him, she gets spooked once again and runs once more. Recognizing that what she needs to do is get in touch with her authentic self, she sets off on a path of discovery. The metaphor for Maggie becoming aware that change needed to happen presented itself in the form of eggs. Maggie did not know her own mind. Her "egg of choice" was based on each of her fiancé's preferred dish. All of the running away was all because she didn't know who she was. She could not show up for anyone else if she was not inherently showing up as her best, most authentic self."

Eggs benedict became the metaphor for Maggie's journey of self-discovery and actualization. Then she was ready to show up for Ike. And, of course, the audience is led to believe she and Ike lived happily ever.

What are some of the choices you make, conscious or unconscious, that lead to your authentic self?

Life in Possessions

The things you choose to bring into your home are a reflection of who you believe yourself to be. They are the journey of you in possessions. Objects speak volumes. They are an extension of yourself as much as words, clothes, and body language. These non-verbal cues also inform others who you are and what you value.

Your Home Is an Extension of Self

Life is fluid; we are always in a state of change. Life giveth and life taketh away. After my father died, I remember walking around my house, removing things, moving things, all in an effort to remind myself that things will never be the same again. Intellectually, I knew that my life would move forward; nonetheless, I had experienced a deep loss. Grief changed me, and my home needed to reflect that significant event. I couldn't possibly walk in and out of that house as if nothing was different. Everything was different. I took my emotions about an event and made a corresponding physical change.

After a divorce, kids leaving home, or any other major lifestyle change, I believe we often need to see the event in some physical form. It anchors us to our "new" reality. We are not who we were. We are changed; therefore, our environment needs to change. I am not talking about an expensive renovation. It could just be a tweak, significant enough that you notice a change has occurred, such as new paint, more/fewer objects, or adding a prominent picture or something you have wanted that you know will make your heart sing when you look at it.

My father had a painting of a light-haired girl with a little turned-up nose standing at the shoreline on a beach holding a shell. He always said it reminded him of me. Frankly, I never saw what he saw in the petite young blond girl's appearance—that she even remotely resembled me—but looking at that painting now in my home brings up such a deep feeling of love. I have become her, or she has become me.

Reimagining your space is especially beneficial after divorce. Often, the property is split and each home looks sparse, like there is something missing. I try to make smaller conversation areas, pick up a few things to "fill the void" if moving is not an option. Don't live in a half-empty house: aim for a look of completion because you are complete just as you are now and moving forward. You are not one half of what used to be a whole, and your home should not reflect that.

Instead, you are the artist painting the masterpiece that is your best life. You are the musician playing musical notes that allow you to vibrate higher. You are the author of your story, penning into reality your magnificent novella. Be mindful of the narrative you have on repeat that—like a broken record—goes round and round playing the same skipped beat. Turn on and tune into your thoughts and deeds. Are you repeating the same mistakes over and over, or are you learning and growing from each failure and accomplishment?

Let's return to my yoga analogy.

The mindfulness that yoga teaches, along with breathwork, are the heart of the practice, unifying the mind, the body, and spirit. I know that when I chant "om" at the beginning of my practice, it settles me. I feel it in my body. It vibrates throughout me. When I am chanting it, I cannot seem to focus on anything else in that moment; nothing else exists. It is symbolically telling my mind and body to settle in and find stillness. I am connecting to myself. I know I arrive at class mostly harried and I leave class relaxed and at peace. It is so simple yet so complex.

There is an analogy between yoga and striving to live mindfully. Living a holistic lifestyle means the unification of mind, body, spirit. I will add and argue that it also includes your living space. When I say living space, I am speaking of your "interior" life, your body, and your environment. All are connected; all are tenets leading us to a happier, healthier, more well-balanced life.

Through my yoga practice, I recognized that the om sound is a part of the word hOMe. I thought that was appropriate, as om represents everything and nothing. It is a vibration and energy just like that of our home.

The word om encompasses a connection between our inner and outer worlds. It is a sacred sound that is known generally as the sound of creation, of the unification of everything in the universe. Om also derives from the belief that vibrations from the chanted sound link back to the vibrations that created the world, reinforcing the reality that everything is energy. It is rooted in the sacred. It connects our inner world to the greater outer and beyond.

The sound appears to have first cropped up in the Upanishads, a collection of sacred texts that inform Hinduism.[3] The *Mandukya*

Upanishad, which is entirely devoted to om, says:

"Om is the universe, and this is the exposition of Om. The past, the present, and the future, all that was, all that is, all that will be is Om."[4]

For such a small word, it is indeed big in meaning. It is a symbol that conveys many meanings: peace, tranquility, and unity. I reference it as the foundation for self-empowering inner and outer peace.

Home, as I describe it here, in this book, is both literal and metaphorical. It is universally integral to our overall well-being. Discovering our om brings us to a place of awareness and stillness within. To achieve that sense of well-being that allows us to reach that place, we need to ask ourselves meaningful questions in an effort to discover who we are authentically, what fulfills us, aligns us, connects us to our higher self. It can't be a coincidence that we find the word om literally within the word hOMe.

When you are happy, healthy, and in balance, it is reflected in your home. The chapters ahead are all about making changes within that will bring greater peace and tranquility to every other aspect of your life.

You'll find the way to:

- Tap into your body to "feel" the answers to life's questions. When you feel good, you will step into your fullest potential and do the things that make your heart sing.

- Look deep within, taking care of all parts of yourself.

- Become an advocate for your own mental, physical, and spiritual well-being.

- Recognize how your home influences and reinforces your self-care and your self-worth.

To create a sacred space—authentic to you—requires a deep dive into your subconscious. Designing your environment from the perspective of reaching our most authentic self takes courage and understanding. The state of your home can tell a lot about the state of your life.

You control everything, big and small. You are in the driver's seat. You are responsible for your own suffering as well as your own well-being.

Let's start by setting an intention to guide you.

Ask yourself:

- Why did you pick up this book? What were you hoping to accomplish?

- Are you looking to make a change in your life? What kind, what does that look like?

- Do you enjoy the process of self-discovery?

- Are you committed to taking steps toward change? Are you open to growth?

- Is there anything that you regularly struggle with?

- Do you consider yourself self-aware? Are you open-minded enough to try new things?

- What are the thoughts that run through your mind the most often? Are they more positive or negative?

- Are you easily set-off or depressed?

- Name your areas of least satisfaction.

– Can you identify triggers that negatively affect you?

TAKEAWAYS:

- Your home is within and outside of you.

- Your home and your health are inextricably tied together.

- Your home should be a reflection of your values and authenticity.

- A growth mindset will get you from where you are to where you want to be.

- When you are living in your purpose, you are living in authenticity. From that comes happiness and fulfillment

- The best way to predict the future is to create it. It's your choice every day!

2

THE BATTLE WITHIN

If you can't fly, run. If you can't run, walk.
If you can't walk, crawl but by all means, keep moving.
—Martin Luther King

ABOUT A YEAR AFTER OUR FIRST SON WAS BORN, my first husband surprised me and bought us a house in a neighborhood that we were sure was the perfect place to bring up children. It was down the street and around the corner from where I grew up. From the moment my husband bought the house, I was ecstatic to move right in and put my design stamp of approval on it.

We had assumed the neighborhood we were presently living in was going to get younger, but we hadn't seen that happening. I was home with a baby without many friends nearby and feeling isolated. So, I was excited about the prospect of buying a newly built home in a newly built development where there were so many other young parents eager to meet each other. I would decorate my new house exactly as I wished, which was a passion of mine at the time, not yet a business. I assumed our new home would be my starter home and my dream home was down the road.

I thought how lucky I was to have such a beautiful starter home, a place to raise my children that felt safe and full of possibility. But I still thought of it as a stepping stone to a stately, stone Tudor home with shimmery copper gutters and a magnificently carved wood-paneled den where the sun shone through the beveled-glass windows, and little prisms of light created dancing rainbows in all directions bouncing off the walls. I could visualize it. I could feel it. It was only a matter of time.

But the house my husband purchased never became just a stepping stone. We stayed. I made many friends that I still call friends to this day, and it became my safe space when my marriage crumbled and I was alone. Looking back, I am so grateful I was able to stay in my home when I was suddenly single again. With so much change, the steadfast security of having my home, where my children felt safe and secure, meant the world to me.

I am still living in that same house I moved into all those years ago. The only thing that has changed has been husbands. I tried to persuade my new husband that we should have a place to call our own. If we were beginning a new chapter together, then our home should reflect both of our wants and needs. "Newness" was an important metaphor for our journey together with a blended family in tow.

I am usually very good at arguing the case for something that is important to me, but not this time. My new husband was having none of it. He was fine to move into what had now become my somewhat generic tract home in a development that seemed tired to me. I was beginning to feel the rub of discontent. Life took its twists and turns, as it does, and time marched on. Our children went off to college, and I was still pining away for something "more me." I had done everything I could do to make a happy, pretty home for us, but there is only so much you can do or only so much money you want to sink into a home that, presumably, will not go up in value or personal appeal.

I felt that my home didn't express me, the person I thought myself to be—original, authentic, creative. The materials are cheap, inauthentic; the homes built by big developers are slapped together quickly and without the participation of tradespeople taking their time to partake in their craft with integrity and honesty. These workers seemed always to have a quota to meet and to rush haphazardly from one home to the next, so that they could then move on to the next development being built.

One day, a few years into my second marriage, I had the opportunity to decorate the living room that had finally outgrown its playroom existence. I dragged my husband to a farm in Upstate New York to buy reclaimed hand-hewn beams excavated from an old barn in Vermont for that "authentically me" living room. If my home wasn't built with distinctive materials and characteristics, I would add them where I could. These beams were the "perfectly imperfect" addition to the white box lacking architectural details that I call home.

Having the beams installed was a bit of a nightmare. When my contractor and electrician were working to resolve weight and wiring issues, they opened up the ceiling. Low and behold, what did they pull out of the opening but a petrified sandwich and an empty bottle of beer. I was furious. What else was lurking between the walls that I was unaware of? Damn this house!

Day in and day out, I longed for a house that didn't look like every other house. Plastic sheds were going up around me; moldy aluminum siding was my reality, playsets that had long rusted were my view. It was hurting my eyes and my heart. I would stop and laugh when the feeling overwhelmed me, recalling that one of my favorite books that I read as a child was *Mr. Pine's Purple House.*

Mr. Pine lived on Vine Street in a little white house. "'A white house is fine,' said Mr. Pine, 'but there are FIFTY white houses all in a line on Vine Street. How can I tell which house is mine?'"[5]

I continued to grow increasingly unhappy. My thoughts around this were creating so much suffering for me. Working on my home with thoughts of improving my situation was proving to fall short, yet it made no sense financially to move to a different home. I understood that, but my thoughts were keeping me in this state of "lack," feeling stuck in my life and feeling so helpless. I blamed the house, I blamed the neighborhood, I blamed the city. I was very busy blaming.

All the same, I knew enough to know that if my living situation was not going to change, the one thing I had control over was the way I thought about the situation. I had to stop the blame game.

I tend to dwell on what bothers me. It might sound silly, but I felt my home had no soul. If my home was a mirror of self, what was my soul saying to me? What did this mean? The inside of my home told a different story. Golden hues gave a soft warmth to my interiors, a touch of animal prints—which I believe is the perfect neutral accent—dotted each room. A dash of drama increased the wow factor—just enough so that the spaces felt exciting but still inviting. The furnishings were comfortable, and the art told a story of my journey thus far.

Inside it felt "like me," and I was happy enough when I would come home and shut the door behind me. But, when I drove through the housing development in disgust, my mind was a barrage of mixed messages. I grappled with trying to be grateful for what I have and simultaneously felt disappointed that I couldn't make the change I so desperately wanted. I was expending a lot of energy, and I made myself exhausted.

Finally, I came to the realization that what I wanted was a different lifestyle. I wanted a bigger life in a world unfamiliar to me. I craved newness, the excitement of discovery, unpredictability, and the opportunity to meet new people. Aha, maybe it wasn't really about the house and was more symbolic of the way I felt. Often, though we may be focused on one thing, a deeper examination reveals that the focus is actually something else. My house represented stagnancy for me.

Since the one thing my husband said "no" to time and time again was moving to another house, I had to retrain my brain to tell myself a different story: A story where happiness and adventure were the theme, not frustration and isolation because I couldn't move. When we are at an impasse between our reality and our thoughts that create suffering around that reality, there is nothing to do but change the thoughts that create the suffering. When you argue with reality, you will never win. You will just drive yourself crazy and suffer more.

I knew I wanted to set my mind free; my thoughts were torturing me, and dissatisfaction was all that I felt. I kept creating for myself exactly what I said I did not want.

"I'll become a life coach," I said one morning, seemingly out of the clear blue. I loved psychology and majored in it in college, but my career path had turned toward fashion instead. I was beginning to feel like I was having a full-circle moment. If I could heal what was not working for me, I knew I could help heal others in some way that had not yet been revealed! The universe must have known what it was doing because I began to see a portion of the picture that the puzzle pieces were revealing. Every day you have a choice to walk a different path if you're not wholly fulfilled.

But, while beginning my life coach education and simultaneously continuing to work as a designer, pursuing an expanded dream, growing, questioning, I noticed I always felt a little "off" physically, a bit more tired than normal. I always had an ache or a pain that lingered a bit too long. I first sought out one doctor, then an army of doctors to hopefully tell me what was wrong so I could fix it. I am a fixer. That's what I do. In interior design, things go wrong all the time. There is always another way to achieve the outcome. We have a plan B and a plan C when plan A fails. All will be well, I told myself—I just have to pivot.

Not this time. I was down for the count. I was diagnosed with and treated for a cadre of issues ranging from Lyme disease to psoriatic arthritis. Systemic inflammation was causing much of the pain and suffering. Throw in a cancer scare and the death of my father, and I was in a dark, unfamiliar place. My hair fell out, and I fell apart. My system was attacking itself, and I felt my body was betraying me.

It became debilitating. I lost interest in many things that had once brought me so much joy. Friends fell by the wayside. I felt isolated and depressed beyond words. All my labs came back normal, and more than a few medical doctors just about told me I was crazy.

"Let me prescribe you depression medication" was something I heard often from traditional doctors.

"I am depressed because I don't feel well," I found myself shouting on more occasions than I care to recall. It was up to me to be my own health care advocate. I sought out doctors of integrative medicine who took a holistic approach to health. Our bodies, our minds, our spirits all play a role.

Let me insert a caveat here. I am all for medication as needed: there is a time and place. What bothered me was that my situation was so unclear, and I did not want to put a band-aid on my condition!

It wasn't lost on me that when your health is off, it can present in a myriad of symptoms, many of them vague and almost always fluid and frustratingly nebulous, as was the case of my autoimmune diagnosis. I wanted to course-correct in a more natural way than pharmaceuticals. For me, that felt like the right approach.

At some point on this journey, it occurred to me that holistic interior design is not unlike holistic health. As a matter of fact, it is not separate from, but is a part of the equation. We need to treat the whole being. The path may look different, but the outcome is similar.

If you feel that something is "off" in your home, you can investigate many areas in your life in an effort to correct what isn't working. If the energy is "less than" ideal, it can relate to any number of factors. Just as negative emotions or illness send signals to the body and the result is pain, an environment that is negative or inauthentic to you can make you feel "off." Your living space is one more pillar of health, one that doesn't get talked about much, but I believe it is equally as important. It's not enough to have a well-designed or well-organized home; you need to be mindful of the energy within—within your body, your mind, and your spirit. There is no one size fits all. We all feel differently, we act differently, we respond differently. We can't always identify what isn't working, but we often know something feels off. It could be our health, it could be our spirit, it could be hidden trauma, feelings of lack, apathy, anything. Regardless, each of us needs to be our own "interior" designer, getting to the root cause of what's off and understanding how to go about correcting it.

While I was lying in bed one day feeling depressed and defeated, I suddenly thought, "Why am I watching such a small TV set deep within an armoire?" The TV was so small that I was having trouble seeing it without glasses, and I was really tired of viewing the inside of the armoire with all its inconsequential contents in full view. I would never set up something like that for a client! How much better would my reality of lying in bed be if I had an amazing TV viewing experience?

I opened my computer and decided on a big, LED, flat-screen TV, and my husband and I were off to the store to "test drive" what was going to be a saving grace. Of course, it can't just hang there in mid-air. A cabinet was necessary to give weight to the wall and balance the TV. I made sure that space was not sacrificed within the chest. Happily, I didn't have to look at the sweaters, mismatched socks, and such that are now housed behind closed doors. A giant crystal amethyst, a pair of black and white splatter ceramic pots my son gave me, and a floral Murano glass vase happily sit on top of an ivory, shagreen sideboard, and I am soothed as I look at it all from my perch in bed.

In making that change, I transformed not only the bedroom environment, but my experience in it on those days when I did not feel well enough to go out.

I had become a warrior. I wanted to be the hero of my wellness journey. Challenges help us grow more fully, and I decided that wellness would become my arrow, held close, and steady determination would be my bow. Whatever physical limitations life threw at me, I would attack head-on with laser focus. Self-sabotaging thoughts became the target. A beautiful alchemy of exploration and self-discovery was taking shape.

This change in my thoughts lowered my stress. I could feel it. I could breathe a little easier. Again, in an effort to fix myself, I was learning more holistic health tools that not only benefited me but could certainly benefit others. I became crystal clear about the interconnection between cause and effect: I improved my environment and my mood improved. Changing the TV did not improve my health, but I was much less miserable when I was in my bedroom. Because I had control of that one small thing, the feeling of control was substantial and my reality more pleasant.

My poor husband. Every time he walked through the door, I was caught red-handed moving things around. I rearranged rooms. I swapped out furniture. I added a few pieces that were in storage and purchased a delicious blanket and oh-so-soft pillows for the sofa. If I had been pregnant, you'd say I was nesting. Instead, I was preparing for my new life: a new and improved life, where I was happy, healthy, and whole because I was willing it into existence.

My mission was to manifest my healthiest, best life. I wanted to shout from the rooftops a message about the importance of space and what you bring into it; how you function within its walls; the shifts you can make—big and small—toward healing; and how to connect your values, expectations, and authenticity to your home.

It was not solely just about a holistic home anymore, but a holistic lifestyle. One does not exist without the other. Like your immune system, the systemic interconnection found within your body, your mind, your spirit, and your space are the foundation on which your health and well-being are built.

Everything is interconnected. Nothing exists alone. Nothing is independent in this world, not a person, not a tree, not a cell. With a change in diet, a change in medicine, a change in my lifestyle, a change in home design, and a change in attitude, I was beginning to take my life back— like a phoenix rising out of the ashes—with renewed vigor and a sense of urgency.

Creating a Holistic Life

Creating a home that nourishes you, that makes you feel safe and that you love to come back to is an amazing gift, but that is only part of the puzzle. To speak of a holistic home is to speak about all the other modalities that have to be in place for you to feel your best and live your best life.

Holism means to see the whole.[6] Different perspectives, different elements, the synergy between the emotional, physical, and spiritual as they all relate to space are interrelated. Can you have good physical health without good emotional health? No, not fully. Can you have a poorly functioning home while having good mental health? Again, the answer would be a resounding no.

There are myriad ways in which we can set our sights on improving areas of our life that may be unsatisfactory.

Holistic Interior Design

A holistic approach to interior design requires us to recognize that everything within us and outside of us is interconnected. Our inner selves are reflected outwardly, and our outward selves are mirrored internally.

Your health is not made up solely of distinct physical and mental components. You are one entity, where mental, emotional, physical, spiritual, and environmental health are connected and multidirectional—meaning one area affects another.

When you apply that perspective of interconnection, of wholeness, of mutualism, whether in the home or in yourself, you are taking a holistic approach to all areas of your life: You have multiple access points for healing and thriving.

Holistic interior design is not about the home alone; holistic design connects the mind, body, and spirit to your environment. It's about the home as part of your entire human experience. It is about a mutualistic relationship where one area can help shine light on another area that needs attention, and both areas—and "the whole"—benefit. For example, the gut has been called the second brain. Much is being studied around how our microbiome can influence what is happening in our body and our brain. This is called the gut-brain axis. There is a deep connection between the two.[7]

There is a vast ecosystem made up of millions of microorganisms residing in our gut. When there is an overgrowth of bad bacteria in your gut or GI tract, which is not as uncommon as you think, an imbalance occurs called dysbiosis:[8] your microbiome is not balanced. Signals are sent throughout the body that there is a threat. Symptoms are observed, ranging from bloating to inflammation to autoimmune disease. If not treated, illness is the result. We are learning the importance of nourishing our bodies to ensure good gut flora. Having a strong mind/body connection ensures that the symptoms you experience elicit a call to action.

When you listen to your body or your mind with openness and compassion, you are able to recognize warning signs and take steps to help heal yourself on a deeper level. There is an alchemy in allowing for the possibility that one area of your life is showing you that another needs attention in order for you to be in better health.

I witnessed this personally through my own health journey. When I put two and two together, I applied the same principles to some of my clients' homes. When there was an imbalance in their life—whether it manifested as an illness, as in the case of a client who had MS, or the client who was mired in high-drama relationships—it always showed up as an imbalance in the energy of the home. You could see it, or you could feel it.

If not treated, illness can be the outcome on an emotional, physical, or spiritual level. That is reflected in phrases such as: having butterflies in your stomach, a gut-wrenching feeling, gut instinct, or the phrase I often use, "I'm having a visceral reaction." These are examples of how we metaphorically or physically tie our gut to our emotional well-being. Once we have the awareness that the connection exists, we can examine the "dis-ease" and set out on a path of wholeness. The path of ease.

If you want to go from not bad or just okay to great, you have to pick an access point, identify something you are dissatisfied with, and apply your effort and energy there. Saying "yes" to that which moves you forward and keeps you aligned to everything that empowers you (as well as saying "no" to everything that detours you or drains you of your energy), allows you to stay on the path to holistic health.

And a part of that path is your home.

Creating a home that nourishes you, makes you feel safe, and that you love to come back to again and again is an amazing gift that is one part of a fairly complicated puzzle. To speak about a holistic home is to speak about your living space as well as all the other modalities that have to be in place for you to feel your best and live your best.

Once you begin to take a holistic approach and heal one area of your life, you will be inspired to improve another area and another area. With each small win, you take steps to climb the next mountain, challenging yourself to be healthier, wealthier, and wiser.

Visualizing your path forward, prepare to move out of your comfort zone, plant a stake, accept what you cannot change. When you are joyful, your whole-body benefits—especially your heart and your mind. In fact, research shows that joyful people have less chance of having a heart attack, have healthier blood pressure, lower cholesterol, better weight management, and decreased stress levels. Also, studies show that happy people are more likely to exercise, eat healthy foods, sleep better, and avoid smoking.[9] Fill your life with joy for better health and well-being!

Ask yourself these questions:

- What kind of food are you fueling up with?

- Do you engage in self-care rituals?

- Are you interested in continuing education?

- Have you created a sense of community so you feel connected to others?

- Do you feel like you are living your life's purpose, or are you chasing a dream?

- Do you have a strong mind-body connection that enables you to go inward for answers to questions that may not be readily apparent?

- Does the constant chatter in your mind ask more questions than it offers answers?

- Do you engage in activities that make your heart sing?

- Are you holding onto things that do not serve your higher self?

- Does your home tell others who you are and what you value?

Remember, you cannot build a home without the proper tools. Similarly, you cannot build a wellness practice without the proper tools. These tools are often learned. If not, we need to discover for ourselves where we need help to heal or grow. We are intuitive creatures. When we feel like something is off, it probably is. With awareness, we can then seek answers.

Perhaps you just never thought to look within the walls of your home—and by that, I mean both your dwelling place and your own body, your ultimate home, your most sacred space. The goal is to be satisfied within yourself and within your home.

Are you dissatisfied in an area of your life?

Where in your life does dissatisfaction lie?

What is the most unsatisfactory place in your home?

You may be surprised that there is a correlation between the inner and the outer lurking in your space. We may show others what we think of ourselves and the way we view the world, but judgments and limiting beliefs can get tangled up within as well. There are messages in the mess, if we know where to look, we can take steps to go about dissolving them.

Have you ever heard the saying: "How you do one thing is how you do everything?" I see evidence of this time and time again. Never was the saying more apt than with my client Victoria, who approached her living space the same way she approached her inner space—by making snap decisions.

Victoria's Story

"But I love him, I am just not sure I can trust him," Victoria said to me over drinks one day. She had a look in her eyes that seemed to say she was trying to convince me more than confirming this affirmation.

"Say more," I said, maybe a little more demanding than curious.

I didn't want to push, but I felt Victoria needed to talk, and I was willing to go where the conversation led. Or, to be honest, maybe I was leading the conversation from that moment on. Regardless, I was determined to get to the root of the problem. Two glasses of wine had made me feel bold.

As a life coach, I'm not supposed to give you answers. Instead, my role is to lead you to ask yourself questions that may, in turn, eventually lead you to an answer that feels true for you. But I wasn't on the clock then. We were just two girlfriends having drinks in a midtown restaurant trying to stay warm one blustery winter night. I cared for Victoria, and I wanted her to have every happiness. She had been through a lot of change over the previous few years.

"At what point does a fiancé, my fiancé, stop looking at other women? His flirting makes me uncomfortable. I've told him that, but it falls on deaf ears."

I asked a question I already knew the answer to.

"This is not acceptable to you?"

"Of course not, aren't you hearing me?" Victoria bemoaned.

"I am hearing you," I shot back. "But are *you* hearing you?"

And that was the aha moment!

Victoria, by anyone's account, appeared to "have it all." She is beautiful, and she lived a fabulous life, wore stunning clothes, went on amazing adventures, and mingled with the who's who at red carpet events. Meeting her, you might immediately want to dislike Victoria because you'd secretly feel envious of her, but you can't because there is an earnestness to her smile. Victoria and I designed many homes together.

But Victoria did have a shadow side, something hiding in plain sight.

I realized that how Victoria does one thing is how she does everything. Victoria rushes. She rushes into relationships, and she rushes into design decisions, and she makes mistakes in both areas. I always say, "There's no substitute for time." There are messages in the mess, and all will be revealed over time.

In the wake of quick decisions, Victoria would get so excited when we were planning a new space that she would inevitably rush out and buy something that would not fit in the room or in the overall plan I was still in the midst of creating.

She'd call me excitedly to tell me about the purchase she had just made, and there was always a push and pull between us. I often had to gently tell her to send it back, or worse, find a place to put it. I have had to redo floor plans more than once. I always begged her to stop and wait until I had a floor plan drawn or measurements confirmed.

Throughout the years we worked together, Victoria was in and out of a couple of marriages. She never did walk down the aisle with said fiancé, but she quickly entered into a new relationship, which imploded in quite a dramatic fashion. She was in a vulnerable place, and I was quite cognizant of creating a new, sacred space for her to heal after the disintegration of that relationship. She had just relocated to a cute little townhouse all her own.

Although the place was small, we had big design ideas with the intention that this was to be a safe haven and a calm refuge. She was always up for a dash of drama, which I loved because that is my specialty. I wanted to paint all the woodwork and cabinetry in her home office in a peacock blue lacquer. This was a perfect choice for Victoria, given where she was in her life. Blue, with the undertone of green, evoking a feeling of calm, immediately making you feel safe and relaxed. It also helps with concentration, which makes perfect sense in a home office. The deep intensity of the peacock hue would punch-up the drama a bit and created a richer, almost regal air. With a giant picture window on the opposite wall, the light reflecting off the high gloss finish would create an energy that I thought Victoria would take a shine to. I had no doubt this design choice would create the perfect feeling we were looking for when feathering this nest.

Lacquering is an age-old technique. This process takes time, patience, and skill. It cannot be rushed. There are steps that need to be followed in order to achieve the incredible durability and shine that only lacquering can accomplish. The paint is generally sprayed or brushed on in many thin coats.

The wood must be properly prepared, then sanded, painted, sanded, painted, sanded, and painted MANY times, building the proper finish. Drying completely between coats is crucial. It is labor-intensive, but, oh, how beautiful the results are in the end.

I was excited that Victoria was on board. I went back to my office and began researching the exact color, as it had to match new upholstered pieces in the room. I wanted to talk to the paint company confirming precise application directions. It didn't occur to me that Victoria would do what Victoria does. Before I could submit all my plans to her, she went rogue and hired a painter herself to paint a high-gloss blue, more royal than peacock, onto the wood—with less than desirable results.

Not two or three weeks old by the time I saw it, the paint already looked chipped in spots, and you could see every blemish in the wood. It had obviously not been prepared properly.

I was so disappointed in this huge fail. I told her what I thought, and this turned out to be her wake-up call—her "come-to-Jesus moment." I expressed that she either had to look inward and make a change or face a life of costly mistakes financially and emotionally, followed by psychological self-flagellation. She was completely unaware of her pattern of behavior.

She vowed things would change. She did a deep dive into her soul. The life she previously led was no longer the one she wanted. She was much more traditional than the life she was leading would have you believe. It was an illusion of who she was, essentially smoke and mirrors. She was not aligned with her authentic self. So, Victoria took a hard look at the mixed messages she was sending out.

Everything changed when she became aligned with her values. She dressed differently, she spoke differently, she surrounded herself with others who accepted her for who she was authentically. Victoria learned to slow way, way down. She became a much more introspective woman, weighing all decisions carefully and intelligently, thinking all decisions through—personal, professional, or otherwise—before acting on them. Victoria lives a quieter life, and she has never been more at peace.

And as for that cabinetry—well, there was no question it all had to be done over. You absolutely cannot have all those blemishes staring back at you, reminding you of past mistakes. It's onward and upward with a fresh coat of paint and a clear vision of what you desire to call into your life.

There is a biblical proverb that says: "*Through wisdom a house is built, and by understanding it is established; by knowledge the rooms are filled with all precious and pleasant riches.*"[10]

It is not enough to have a well-designed home anymore—we must be mindful of the "riches" within our thoughts, our behavior, our relationships, and our environment, as well as of the self-talk we use to help or harm. None of this is separate.

If our outer space mirrors our inner space, then a cluttered house equals a cluttered mind. If our inner space mirrors our outer space, a peaceful mind equals a peaceful home.

Designing a harmonious life full of rich relationships, balance, and living in authenticity is interdependent upon designing a home that:

- Is aligned to support your desires

- Facilitates healthy relationships

- Reduces stress

- Supports healthy habits

- Enables you to manifest the things you want in life.

Your life should be built upon the goals you set for yourself and the values you hold dear: the who you envision yourself to be, the who you aspire to be at your CORE.

AT THE C-O-R-E OF EVERYTHING

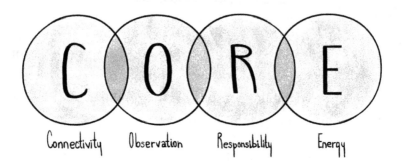

Connectivity: understanding that everything is interconnected. Your emotional, spiritual, intellectual, physical, environmental, even financial well-being are each pillars of wellness, one dependent on the other. The connection between your talent, your knowledge and your experiences give rise to being in purpose. When you are in purpose, you are fulfilled. When you are fulfilled, you are in full bloom.

You cannot have a well-designed home that supports a healthy lifestyle while your mind is full of negative thoughts or negative energy. You cannot have a healthy home if you are unhappy and questioning what you are meant to do.

Your home cannot be healthy if it's filled with toxic chemicals, just as you cannot have a healthy body if it's filled with processed food and excess sugar. It is important not to engage in toxic relationships as well. Even if you dwell in an immaculate house, those things will be at odds with one another. Inner and outer peace, inner and outer beauty, inner and outer health—they go hand in hand. One cannot exist without the other.

Observe: self-observation is critical for transformation, which begins with awareness. Having the observational skill set to practice self-observation means noticing what you are thinking, feeling, doing, and imagining to become self-aware. When you are aware of what you are thinking, feeling, doing, and imagining, you realize that you have choices, and choices are what make us powerful. When you practice self-observation, you will begin to recognize that the part of you doing the observing is your true self. Having that self-awareness allows you to see when you are behaving in alignment with your goals and your values and when you are not. You can also recognize when your choices are serving you and when they are not.

Responsibility helps you recognize that *only you* can be in control of yourself. You are responsible for your thoughts, your beliefs, your emotions, your home, your health. How you react to the ever-changing landscape over your "interior" ensures more enjoyment in your life, not just endurance. And, taking personal responsibility for choices and actions not only makes you accountable for yourself, but allows for relationships with deeper understanding, trust, and compassion.

You are not what happens to you, you are what you make of what happens to you. Being able to see that your decisions have a direct impact on your life's events is what being able to accept personal responsibility is all about.

Energy is everywhere. Everything is energy. We are more than physical matter. We consist of energy; our homes consist of energy—different states of being emit different energetic frequencies. You can feel it and empower yourself to control your personal energy with your thoughts. Nothing has meaning unless you give it meaning with your energy. Your thoughts created by energy create a specific vibration (whether you are aware of it or not), and that energy will seek out its vibrational match, and your home is an extension of that.

When you are vibrating at your magnificent best, you are attracting others who are vibrating at their magnificent best. Think about what can be accomplished when you are all energetically in tune at your highest level.

Call it magical thinking, but in these challenging times, among challenging people, along with our challenging thoughts, it is more important than ever to nurture yourself and create a sanctuary that calms you (within and outside of yourself) and centers you every time you walk through that door.

Could you be better, more joyful, more balanced, more connected to your inner wisdom? Can you do better, listen to your body and give it what it needs to succeed? Can you accept the things you cannot change in a healthy way, understanding that everything happens for a reason, even if we don't know what that reason is? Can you detach from the stories you tell yourself that you believe to be true? Can you let go of what no longer serves you?

Clutter shows up in our lives in a myriad of ways. In our home, absolutely; in our minds, no doubt; in our body, science suggests it is so. Female undergraduate students chose cookies over carrots and crackers as a snacking option when they were placed in a cluttered kitchen environment or asked to recall a time when they had an out-of-control mindset. The study suggests a cluttered environment or cluttered mindset may create a sense of vulnerability.[11]

I know this to be true from personal experience. The first winter I rented an apartment in Florida, it was bright and cheerful-looking. My sightline was over the palm trees swaying in the wind. I opened my blinds each morning and jumped out of bed, eager to exercise, then make myself a delicious green smoothie for breakfast. I felt great and was noticeably happier. The following winter in my townhouse rental, it was darker and noisier than I would have liked. I felt cramped and claustrophobic. I remember eating more sugar-laden foods that season. I lacked the enthusiasm of the previous year. I realized it while standing over the sink eating a peanut butter and jelly sandwich for dinner one night. What had this environment done to me?

Clearing clutter and emotional blocks leads to abundance. Abundance leads to more fulfillment. Fulfillment leads to contentment. It is a beautiful cycle of shedding and creating, a continuous cycle of metamorphosis, as we adapt, fine-tune, and try to maintain what is good for us on our path to discovering our best selves. Be the hero of your own wellness journey. You owe it to yourself. Follow your intuition, pay attention to your body's inner intelligence, let go of negativity, lean into soul desire, and a kind of magic takes place.

Some of the happiest people on the planet live in the Nordic or Scandinavian region of the world, but the Danes stand out as the happiest group and have the highest feeling of life satisfaction.[12] Many of the reasons they are happier have to do with their lifestyle choices and how they decorate and interact in their home. The Danes believe their home should reflect the little things that bring comfort and joy and strive to achieve that daily.

There is a sensuousness to textiles, sights, sounds, smells, all pleasurable. Your home should envelop you, like a warm hug with good energy, cleanliness, and beauty. There is a coziness, a feeling of intimacy and safety within. You create an atmosphere that allows for joyful experiences, alone or with friends and family. The Danes have a word for this; *hygge* (hoo-guh).[13]

The closest English translation is "cozy." To be cozy is to be content. It is even described as "coziness of the soul."[14] The word hygge originated from the Norwegian word *huggu,* which means "to comfort."[15] Hygge and well-being or happiness became intertwined. It is hard to explain but easy to feel. That cup of tea by a crackling fire: hygge.

The wafting scent of a freshly made meal as family comes in after a long day, and you feel your heart leap at the sight of them: hygge. Rising in the morning and swinging your legs off the bed and feeling your feet swallowed up by the plush feel of a thick sheepskin carpet on a cold morning: hygge. Reading side by side with your lover, content and present: hygge.

There is no such thing as a cluttered space if you're living hygge because organization is a priority. Gathering around a common focal point like a TV or a fireplace, where in essence you are creating a sense of intimacy within a larger space: that, too, is hygge. Anyone can incorporate the spirit of hygge into their life. The Swedes also subscribe to this cozy way of living. They call it *mys* (mees). Mys is more about putting hygge into action.[16] You know you have achieved it if you feel good in your own skin and in an environment. You are free to be your best self because you are present and feel fulfilled. No matter what word you use, the importance of creating surroundings that make you feel good and give you pause to think about what's truly important is universal.

Developing a mindful pursuit of wellness and balance must include the impact of home on your psyche.

"We shape our buildings; thereafter they shape us."—Winston Churchill[17]

One conversation that has come out of the pandemic is the realization that we, singularly and as a population, need to slow down. Home is ground-zero when living a hygge lifestyle. Being in your happy place, body, mind, soul, and space is a God-given right that we all have, but it is not given to us. We must create it. We must understand ourselves so well that we know what we need and how to attain that which personally enriches us. Our well-being is a daily choice.

What kind of transformation could you make internally or outwardly that will enhance your life going forward, to consciously design a life full of happiness and success? Be an advocate for your wellness journey! Set and reach goals! Rise to your highest potential! You have the power within you to do it.

Having a home that supports your overall well-being is the intersection where inner peace meets outer beauty. You are on the path to living your best life with intention and purpose. That's what I call "Living BeautiFULLY!" Think of it as a makeover for your home and your heart, and decorate accordingly.

TAKEAWAYS:

- Creating a healthy, holistic home that feels authentic to you requires the desire and implementation of tools to get to the root of who you are, what you believe, and how you behave.

- Study your CORE pillars of wellness and how they apply to you.

- Big and small changes can have a dramatic effect on how you see the world and your role in it.

- Identify areas in your life that you question, that you are dissatisfied with, that you wish were different in some way.

- Do you feel stuck? How? It's a mindset.

- What do you value? When you live by your personal set of values, you become unshakable.

- Who are you authentically?

Let's begin to uncover some of the answers to these questions.

3

IMPRINTED PAST

Your sacred space is where you find yourself over and over.
—Joseph Campbell

CAN YOU CLOSE YOUR EYES AND REMEMBER A FORT or castle you built as a kid? Was it rough-and-tumble or bright and sparkly? Was it made on the fly or designed as a calculated enclosure? Did you use it as a hideout to get away from your siblings or parents, perhaps with a "No Boys Allowed" sign? Or was it an inclusive space, home to Barbies and fantasies that the neighborhood kids could participate in? Picture it. Can you recall the details—the smells, the sounds, the feeling that came over you when you were playing there? The freedom?

Early memories of having a safe space to play and to be yourself is every child's rite of passage. It's one of the first things you do that begins to establish boundaries and creates an independent place for yourself.

As you get older and your humble blanket forts become something grander, they hold more than your prized treasures of childhood. It is here that you're beginning to shape your environment.

It's No Accident that I Love Beautiful Things

I grew up in a home with beautiful art and antiques, fashion-forward furniture, every corner with a vignette curated by my creative mother. She dabbled in interior design. At one time, she painted. She cooked delicious meals with a pinch of this and a dash of that, creating something from nothing. These things came naturally to her, like they later came naturally to me. Some might have considered our Tudor-style home fancy because it was designer-decorated, but it was all very livable; no space was off-limits, with little hiding spaces tucked in on each floor that we fantasized only "us kids" knew about.

We also had a home in the Pocono Mountains for much of my childhood and early teen years. It was similarly designed to be lived in. It was a Bavarian-style home, with intricate gingerbread carvings that had a Hansel and Gretel quality to it in a little village among other Bavarian-style homes of different sizes and colors. The environment was whimsical and idyllic.

Back then, we were free to play outside all day, and I had my "mountain friends"—boys and girls of similar ages from all types of backgrounds, whose families each owned a home in this little village. There was a horse stable at the bottom of the hill—which seemed so big to a child—and at the top of the hill was a lake at the foot of a mountain. That hill between the lake and the mountain loomed large. In the summer, it served as a concert space and had the perfect pitch for tumbling and for movies under the stars. In the winter, it was the first and best ski slope to master before moving on to the mountain.

We felt so free! We used our imaginations in ways that seem like time has forgotten: building forts and catching salamanders under big rocks after rain had saturated the ground, then building elaborate terrariums for newts or snakes or other reptiles. My terrarium always included a house-like structure, a water feature, some kind of exercise apparatus—either a stick with an interesting shape or a series of pebbles connecting one living space to another. I'd add plants for height and visual interest, maybe a small sand dune, if I thought the turtle or salamander would approve.

After supper, we would drag our sleeping bags out to our forts and sleep under the stars some nights; on others, I would lie in my bedroom, which was in the back of our two-story Bavarian-style home with the gingerbread trim, listening to the sound of water trickling over the rocks in the creek not 100 feet away. I can still hear the sound of the stream and that trickling sound it made as it flowed slowly in the drier months, and the rushing, urgent sound it made during the summer rains.

I can smell the earthy aroma of the woods mixed with the humidity hanging in the air after a warm rain. I ran through the verdant greenery—tall grasses and the creeping mint that grew roughshod over the grass in the fields, releasing its cool, aromatic smell.

So, you see, it is also no accident that I became a designer, or that my favorite color is green. Whether it is a natural piece of wood furniture or a perfectly balanced vignette of accessories living in harmony with one another, these things were imprinted on me long ago. My artist's eye seeks out beauty. I am someone moved by a rustic and refined aesthetic.

A bit of the color green ties rooms together in my home, and having an antique in a room lends the patina and the tension necessary for me to feel truly comfortable. There are those hand-hewn beams in my living room and hardwood floors throughout. These things bring me joy.

I need the respite of mountains to feel balanced when life closer to the city feels too hectic. As much as the mountains call to me, the ocean calls to my husband. He grew up a mile and a half from the beach with his toes in the sand and the salty, sweet smell of the ocean permeating every childhood memory he has. But for me, my strong emotional attachment is to the dusty, wooded trails and the sight of the mountains' snow-covered peaks. That's because my happy childhood experiences reside there.

Finding ways to honor both of us is the part of relationship-building that takes into account the art of compromise and respect for one another's sensory triggers. We may actively alternate spending time between the beach and the mountains. More metaphorically, our home has touches of pale ocean blue and lush woodland green.

I do the same when designing for multiple people who reside together in a home. Each is considered and honored to keep ties to the past while moving into the future together.

Past Places Inform Present Spaces

We more often than not think in terms of aesthetics when we consider the decor of our homes. What do we like or not like? What colors are pleasing to our eye? What style of home appeals to us? What is being touted as the latest and greatest? A good designer is not a trend follower, nor should any good client be a trend follower. It tells me you don't know yourself well enough to make selections for your home based in authenticity. We are constantly evolving, and our home should follow suit. There is much more at play. There is a psychological effect that you may not be aware of. Think about the look you naturally gravitate toward. Keep in mind that your aesthetic evolves as you evolve. What you once loved, you may grow tired of. What once served you no longer does as you move through life stages; you require your home to function differently. Life is fluid. We are fluid. Tastes change; life is a series of changes, and we need to honor that in our sacred spaces. We gravitate to what speaks to us on a deeper level. We need to know what that is. Where does it come from? What should we be buying? How should our homes look? Are we wasting time? Did our past experiences already influence our decision making? The answer is yes and no. And it can be found in the study of environmental psychology.

Environmental Psychology

Environmental psychology relates to the interplay between people and their environments. Environmental psychologists seek to understand how and why your environment impacts you and how you can leverage that knowledge to your advantage. It is the interplay between people, their environment, and the world at large.[18] The goal is to discover how and why your environment impacts you the way it does in order to optimize your most positive state of well-being within that environment. It emphasizes the importance of the connection between your environment and your overall health.

I believe it is more intuitive than intellectual when we follow our emotions and listen to the voice within. Environmental psychology also asks: "How do you affect your environment?" Each influences the other, and round and round it goes. It's like the chicken and the egg. Where does it begin? Who's to say?

If you are attuned to the connection between your mind and body, you will notice the cues and act accordingly. You know how a space makes you feel, but often you may not give it a thought. I'd like to change that, and in turn, change the trajectory of your well-being as a whole.

Our past places inform our present spaces. The ties that bind us to cherished spaces and happy childhood memories ground us. Our emotional architecture or environmental "rootedness" is built upon this foundation.

These places shape our sense of identity as profoundly as ancestors in a family tree. Environmental memories of "place attachment"[19] come with a lot of mixed emotions. Sensory cues of early environments are powerful triggers that deeply affect our intimate spaces, spaces that have the power to heal or harm us. Our childhood dwelling is where we first got in touch with our ego selves, when we were forming our identity and our relationship to our environment. Looking back at these places that hold strong memories helps us understand ourselves more deeply as adults. It can be a richly textured experience to unearth how you have recreated a sense of place that is rooted in childhood.

In Dr. Toby Israel's book, *Some Place Like Home: Using Design Psychology to Create Ideal Places*, Dr. Israel contends that past attachments to childhood places are environmental autobiographies or genealogical treasure chests that contain important clues about gathering our story of self.[20] It is said that your grandparent's home holds special meaning: a safe haven, a space that you often unconsciously tap into when you begin making a home of your own. Grandparents, whose role it is to support parents, have much influence and are seen as the roots of a family. Their homes represent a place of unconditional love, fun, and adventure without the constraints of discipline, punishment, homework, or rules that many of us associate with the homes we grew up in.

Understanding your past leads to understanding your present. We know that applies to our thoughts, behaviors, and beliefs, but did you know it also includes your attachment to past places? This information can help you design an environment that is wholly enriching. We have to be crystal clear about what memories, attachments, and values to call forth to ensure comfort and joy.

The Apple Doesn't Fall Far

I posed an exercise to one of my clients, asking her to recall her grandmother's home, knowing she was especially close to her. Did she mimic any kind of design aesthetic in her own home that she recalls from her grandmother's?

"Absolutely not," was her response. Her grandmother loved jade plants, both figuratively and literally, and modern Danish furniture that my client deemed "uncomfortable." My client told me she did not like her ancestor's taste, which is why she went (or so she thought) in the opposite direction when decorating her own home.

I laughed out loud.

"What's so funny?" she said as I looked around her house. I was standing in the great room of her open-concept ranch home with its quintessentially 1950s era terrazzo flooring and floor-to-ceiling wall of windows.

There were two seating areas, one with an atomic-era coffee table between an Eames chair and a sofa, all in an iconic 1950s design vibe that is indicative of the mid-century modern look she had just told me was her goal for the design of her home, a design rooted in functionality, ease, and simplicity.

When I walked through the giant red doors of her home, which featured an imposing Asian knocker and coordinating hardware: I was immediately greeted with an atrium in the foyer. Within its octagonal glass frame, there was a small Zen rock garden with a few plants asymmetrically giving weight to one corner. It was all quite beautiful and had good energy, not unlike the contemporary interpretation of what looked like a sculpture of a jade plant in a jeweled pot that my eye was drawn to nearby.

I pointed out that the jade plant symbolizes good luck and fortune. The crassula ovata with its fleshy, succulent-like evergreen leaves calls forth wealth, especially by an entrance. *"Jade by the door, poor no more*," as the ancient proverb goes.[21]

While she did not literally replicate the design choices of her parents and grandparents, there was most certainly a "flavor" to her choices that resonated from her past. She suddenly had a flashback to an Eero Saarinen tulip table and chairs that she remembered dining from, and she became really impassioned.

My client was emotionally triggered when she recalled this cherished memory. She could describe how she felt in that environment, what it smelled like, familiar sounds associated with that time in her life with her grandmother, down to the tiniest detail of the décor.

She called me two days later and excitedly told me that she had always loved and was thrilled that her house included a somewhat rugged screened-in porch where she often entertained. It has double doors that clack a certain way each time they close.

She just assumed she liked it because she liked it, but after our little exercise, she realized that it connected her to her carefree camp summers spent in Maine. Each time she hears that sound, it gives her a little thrill with the knowledge of this connection.

She told me I had helped her uncover a part of herself she didn't even realize existed, which gave her a whole new perspective on her home, one that filled her with more joy and set her at peace within its walls.

When our "feel-good triggers"—all the things that bring you pleasure or make you feel good—do not match our expectations or present reality, you might find yourself unfulfilled, unhappy, or feeling stuck. Understanding what our soul seeks and giving in to that as best as you can allows for a more blissful state.

Surrounding yourself with things that are representative of warm memories carried over from childhood is certainly one way to connect your environment to your authentic self. This is naturally part of your story.

I have worked with individuals who have not carried forth any characteristics of remembered childhood homes because their past homes held negative triggers. We need to figuratively shed the weight of emotions that might be brought up, and that's okay. That's perfect. We recognize that the emotional bonds we hold are not necessarily good for us or something we get pleasure recreating.

I always tell clients, "It is as important to know what you don't want as it is to know what you do." Messages for how to move forward are derived from both, and accessing the awareness is where it begins.

What Childhood Memories Have You Carried Forward?

Activity 1.

Make a list of positive adjectives that describe (or you would like to describe) your ideal environment. Do these descriptive words apply to your current living space?

- Where would you consider your happy place? Why? What makes it your happy place? What connects you there?

- What makes your heart sing?

- Look at your list of all the positive, joyful, heart-racing, pulse-pounding adjectives that bring you happiness. Can you incorporate more of these "feel good" elements in your home?

Activity 2.

Make two columns.

- In the first column, list all the happy memories you have from childhood relating to an environment.

- In column two, list anything that you have consciously or (up until now) subconsciously incorporated into your home that is similar to something in column one.

- Connect the items in the columns with lines in order to really see the connections.

Did anything surprise you?

Is there anything that brings you pleasure when you think about it: a happy memory that you can in some way incorporate into your environment now? What feelings are associated with these environmental cues?

If you asked me where I'd ideally see myself living, I would have said New York City. I love the energy, the multitude of options, the design community, the culture, the restaurants, the walkability, the shopping of the city. I could go on and on. BUT, when I think about the adjectives that describe what makes my heart sing and makes me feel deeply calm and nourished, that place is quiet, woodsy, and filled with light.

There is a disconnect between what I say I want and what I know will make me feel my best. I am assuming I would ultimately be unhappy in New York, but I'll never know because the universe had other plans for me.

I now see that we get what we need. We don't always get what we want, but that was a long, disappointing lesson to learn. This is where learning to let go, and trust comes in.

Many people fuel a fire burning within when they do not listen to their soul, and they move away from what their inner voice is telling them. Another name for this is intuition. That little "voice" or a gut instinct that keeps you on the right path, that is knowing. After all, it always brings us back to a feeling state. We feel the heat of the embers and recognize that something is ignited, but unfortunately, for many, until we get burned, we do not act. The question is, how can we have both what we want and what we need? The home that connects us to our higher self feeds us body, mind, and soul. Everything falls into place when we come to it authentically and without resistance.

TAKEAWAYS

- Consider how and why your environment looks and the way it does, and how it makes you feel. Can you trace it back to anything from your past?

- Bringing forth good memories through design connects you to your past and is healthy. Anything that connects you to negativity should be released.

- Your home must unite you to your higher self. You must know what that is.

- Intuition will rarely steer you in the wrong direction.

- Trust the process and trust that we get what we need.

4

THE CLUTTER CONVERSATION

You can tell what you build your self esteem around
based on the things you hold onto.
—Amy Morin

By now, you've probably heard about and taken in the advice of Marie Kondo, absorbing her "Konmari Method." Kondo became a sensation after writing the *New York Times* best-selling book, *The Life-Changing Magic of Tidying Up.* The book suggests that you organize your belongings category by category and ask yourself, "Does this spark joy?"[22] Clutter clearing is always the first step because only after you have "tidied" can you go within and begin to ask questions about what brings you joy and reflects your authenticity.

You may "spring clean" all year long or become an organizational wizard with a Pinterest-worthy pantry, or have bathroom essentials beautifully displayed under the sink and categorized by size and color with pretty labels attached. Visually stunning, it easily could leave others a bit intimidated by the level of commitment it takes to purchase, catalog, and maintain all of that. It is a skill worth having, however. You have undoubtedly heard that the more you declutter, the more you allow the feeling of abundance to enter your life. You understand the concept. The decluttering craze is so strong that charities are becoming overwhelmed with used items, and recycling centers are turning people away.[23] The popularity of public storage centers is on the rise. Consignment stores are filled to the brim.

All that decluttering and organizing still may not be enough, though. We may be parting with our possessions, but how long before we fill the space back up again? How long before our well-intentioned, magnificently awe-inspiring closet is a mess? What is the deeper meaning? What is the root cause of this condition, and how is it related to our body, our mind, our spirit?

Do you live in a state of clutter?

1. Does your home feel cluttered to you?

2. Do you feel chaotic or calm?

3. Do you have drama in your life—kids, friends, or work that takes up a lot of headspace?

4. Are you feeling resistance in any area of your life?

5. What fears do you have? Are they real?

6. Do you engage in self-sabotaging behavior?

7. Do you think others would identify your home as cluttered?

8. Do you have trouble purging things?

9. Do you have trouble finding things?

10. Do you love and respect your home?

11. Do you love and respect yourself?

12. Is everything "in its place?"

13. Are you an action-oriented person?

14. Do you only bring things into your home that you love, need, or want?

15. Are there any places in your home that feel oppressive, make you feel uncomfortable?

16. Are there areas in your home you avoid?

17. Are repairs up to date?

18. Can you say, "My home is light, bright, and makes me happy?"

My Home Is CLUTTERED

Robert was a single man who needed help sorting through some clutter and was interested in updating a few areas in his home. I was called in as an interior designer, or so I thought. I had trouble getting past the front door. I was met with so much stuff.

My first impression of what was obviously once a beautiful, fairly large, angular contemporary wood home with lots of windows and a yard with great potential, was today one of complete heaviness. Beyond the door and my client was complete chaos. Items were stacked in front of me like sentinels warning me like a giant neon "do not enter" sign, to go no further. It was hard for me to move forward physically as well as emotionally.

Boxes in his foyer were filled with possessions that once belonged to his parents, whose home he'd cleared out long ago after they passed away. There were many awkward and superfluous items, including art collected over their lifetimes, leaning one against another on a wall. You couldn't step into the hallway without dodging the giant protruding pile. Vending machine inventory from a previous business stood like an army of soldiers at the ready on either side of the doorway, raising a huge red flag. Seemingly random items were abandoned on every horizontal surface: remnants of 30 years of life as a husband, father, then post-divorce. It was difficult to get to the bedroom and impossible to use the kitchen.

Traffic patterns were impossible to navigate due to a lack of space. No clear path allowed movement from room to room throughout the home. The kitchen was not available for use because every surface was "in use" as a placeholder for more stuff. How was he even nourishing himself? Wherever you looked, there was a hodgepodge of miscellaneous paraphernalia: old newspapers and magazines, collectibles of all kinds, broken household items long ago abandoned, all buried beneath more stuff. The home felt stuck in a time warp calling out for more than a good cleaning. Dare I say Robert was a hoarder.

According to the Anxiety and Depression Association of America, hoarding is defined as "the persistent difficulty in discarding or parting with possessions regardless of their actual value."[24] A lack of functional living space was a consistent theme throughout the house and is common among hoarders, who may also live in unhealthy conditions. This was a chaos of the highest order.

I explained that before we tackled the house, coaching was in order. As I got to know Robert better and felt comfortable asking him probing questions that he was emotionally ready to answer, it became clear to me that Robert's home was a metaphor for his heart. He talked of wanting a relationship, but past hurts loomed large and kept him from pursuing another love interest. Robert's emotional baggage turned to physical baggage that was too heavy to drag around.

The clutter at the front door was more than a metaphor. It literally stopped you in your tracks, preventing you from moving forward. I saw it and felt it plain as day. I needed to get Robert to see it, too. There was no way Robert could bring a woman into this situation, and if he did, she would have sensed a problem at the front door. He had a beautiful home with lots of potential, but it was dated, and Robert was living in the past.

He talked about the cost of the custom furniture and built-ins he had made for the house long ago and how the thought of tearing it all out and updating things was out of the question. He had an irrational attachment to his stuff, but he was sabotaging himself, using his stuff as an excuse to not move on with his life.

Psychologically Speaking

There may be feelings of shame or vulnerability attached to those living this way. We can clean the clutter, but if we don't get to the root of the problem, it won't be long before new clutter takes its place or a different destructive behavior rears its ugly head. Getting to the root of any problem ensures a healthy recovery.

For someone who has difficulty throwing things away, there is real anxiety and fear attached to the concept of discarding things. Hoarding, or the act of extreme accumulation, sometimes presents when someone has problems with indecisiveness, has experienced trauma, or has an emotional attachment disorder.[25] The accumulation of things may refocus someone's attention away from an underlying issue. It is not a clutter problem; it is a perception or thinking problem.

It is rooted more in an obsessive-compulsive disorder than addiction, but I have heard these used interchangeably. There is no one real cause for this behavior but a multitude of contributing factors, which makes it hard to resolve without a combination of therapies. I have noticed people who suffer from it attempting to compensate for a perceived "lack." After all, they may need (fill-in-the-blank) one day.

But the hoarder really has a diminished quality of life. Robert would have argued that was not true, but he'd be wrong. We use self-sabotaging behavior as a form of control. We can control our environment even if it is not healthy. No one can hurt us because we are hurting ourselves. Ironically, we end up manifesting exactly what we do not want. We'll go down in flames, but it is a fire of our own making. It's similar to an obese person who keeps weight on to keep a relationship at bay, the compulsive shoplifter who has plenty of money, or the insecure romantic who will sabotage a relationship.

Attempting to move forward while living in a home that is carrying the energy of the past is impossible. Fresh energy begets fresh starts. Robert's home needed to be decluttered, cleaned, and updated. Once Robert became aware and sought help for why he was behaving this way, with awareness came the ability to make a change. When we know, we can grow and let it go!

Robert needed to rid himself of the negative thinking and limiting beliefs about relationships that were keeping him stuck in this thought pattern so he could step into his future in a healthy, positive way. Growth and a successful relationship after a failed one is most certainly possible. After compassionate listening, thought work, and space clearing, cleaning, and a fresh coat of paint, I am happy to report Robert has reconnected with the love of his life, and I hear there is talk of marriage. I surmised that Robert's "accumulation" behavior was a safety mechanism, but love also could give you that feeling in a healthier way, no?

There is no doubt in my mind that when Robert understood how his thoughts around love and intimacy were manifesting, and he took baby steps to clear blocks, change his mindset, declutter, and clean, it became easier to overcome his feeling of "overwhelm" that had been building up. Setting yourself up for small wins leads to big change (and possibly the love of your life).

The Metaphor Exercise

It may sound silly, but giving something a name makes it feel more manageable. It's a way to take the power out of it. If you can name "the thing"—the emotion or the physical presence—you can engage with it in a more concrete way. It is an alternative way to view a situation.

Metaphors allow us to communicate complex or abstract thoughts in a way that helps us visualize a path forward. In this case you could metaphorically address the house as Sloppy House rather than a giant, messy, no-name situation. You will also be able to break down tackling Sloppy House into actionable steps that you can use when you interact with any problem. You can apply this technique to any situation.

We are basically creating our own metaphor for a problem and attempting to solve the metaphor in the hope of solving the problem at hand. This is a skill that takes time. Try it on; keep trying it until you get more comfortable with the metaphor tool. This exercise is playful, don't take it too seriously; use stream of consciousness when coming up with your metaphor.

If you are becoming overwhelmed with life, love, children, what-have-you, and the telltale signs are showing up as clutter and mayhem in your home, and in your life:

STOP, go inward, and ask yourself:

- What am I feeling? Be specific. Where in your body is it registering? For example, "My chest feels constricted." Or, "It feels like a noose around my neck." Also, a great metaphor, by the way. What would it take to, inch by inch, loosen the rope's grip around your neck?

- Ask yourself, "How did I get here?"

- Where do these feelings stem from?

- Give your feelings or the issue a name. For example, if you are feeling overwhelmed and your house is sloppy, you can call it Sloppy House, as I did in this example.

- Talk about the issue, using the term you have named your feelings.

- Visualize Sloppy House, smell it, feel it in your bones. Leave no stone unturned in your mind recalling every detail of Sloppy House.

- Literally, talk to your metaphor. *"Sloppy House, why have you shown up? What are you here to show me/teach me? How can we work together to resolve Sloppy House and make you and me feel heard?"*

Perhaps Sloppy House feels neglected because you haven't shown it the love it feels it deserves. By not respecting it with cleanliness or organization or your own self-care, it fell into disrepair because it was being loyal to you. Sloppy House felt invisible, disrespected until you recognized Sloppy House was always there protecting you, keeping you safe, waiting for you to return the love it was showing you year after year after year. Sloppy House was saying, "When you take care of you, I know you will take care of me. I was just waiting for you to realize it."

Once you become aware that Sloppy House was crying out for attention, you made repairs, created curb appeal, designed a better-balanced environment, repainted and, in return, gave yourself the priceless gift of awareness to move toward personal growth because now Sloppy House, in all its new-found, gleaming glory, signals to you that it is time for you to transform, too. It is a symbiotic relationship.

When life becomes stressful, a situation can seem overwhelming, so trying to tackle it head-on, even if it feels too difficult, will lead you to understanding. Big risk equals big reward. If you turn your troubles into a visual metaphor, an image that you, the viewer, is meant to understand as a symbol for something else, it helps you organize your thoughts and visualize a solution.

Here are a few more examples: the old ball and chain, caught in a spider's web, drowning in quicksand, circling the drain. All these familiar examples of metaphors help you visualize the big picture, but you can create any metaphor that comes to you, then allow yourself the space to pull it apart in small, digestible increments in order to make sense of your perceived struggle.

Even if you feel you've taken those first steps toward separating yourself from the emotional weight that your "stuff" was causing, ironically, *any* overabundance of stuff leads to a feeling of lacking abundance. We are overwhelmed by our stuff. Having more does not lead to happiness or fulfillment.

Often, you think that if I only had this or that—then maybe I would be happy, maybe I would feel fulfilled, and my life would be better. Yet, most of us know intuitively that fulfillment comes from within. This is different but related to accumulating too much of anything or hanging on to the past.

We never find what we are searching for outside of ourselves from the things we buy or fill our homes with.

Any kind of excess consumption is too much consumption. It doesn't matter if we are talking about too much stuff, consuming too much food, or engaging in too much drama in our relationships. Across the board, one affects the other.

When people begin to see that they can have an effect on their lives in one area, they begin to take action in other areas of their life, too, because everything is interconnected.

And so, on your path to putting the om in your home, a *deeper* dive is absolutely necessary, one of the mind.

Negative space—that space where nothing exists—is where you are free to explore mind, body, spirit. In the void or stillness is where answers come; it is where you are free to question and grow. In translating that to home, sometimes when I go into a client's home, I let them know I'm going to take away a few things—that in the empty space lies beauty. When each object is given consideration, like each thought, our mind has the freedom to make better sense of it.

There is so much to uncover as you empower yourself on your path to holistic wellness. All four elements—body, mind, spirit, and living space—need to be considered because none stands alone. None exists in a vacuum. Each influences the other.

Understanding the importance of all these elements and how they work together synergistically can take you from overwhelmed to overjoyed. Having your home support such om is my ultimate hope for you.

It Begins with the Chi

There are those things that you can see, and there are those things that you can feel. You feel rather than see energy, but it makes as great an impact as anything you can perceive with your eyes. For example, some homes are seemingly neat, but you can still feel a heaviness looming. This indicates something called "stuck energy." The "chi" is not in balance.

Chi is an ancient Chinese word meaning "universal life force" or "universal energy."[26] It flows through all of creation. Everything is made up of this dynamic, vibrating energy. When chi is correctly harnessed, you are balanced, focused, and in good health in your body, mind, spirit, and living space.

Chi is expressed in many forms and in both positive and negative energies; your goal is to create harmony within yourself, between people, and within spaces.

We are a mirror of our surroundings. I have been in clients' homes and have witnessed firsthand the correlation between the state of their home and the state of their mind. The drama or toxicity overflows from life into home, home into life when we are living with unhealthy behavior patterns. Clutter and disorganization of the mind equals clutter and disorganization in the home and, sometimes, between people in a home.

The Clutter Effect

The "clutter effect" is a term used to describe how clutter affects everything from stress to life satisfaction to cognition.[27] Clutter is a teacher presenting us with a lesson. Clearing the clutter allows room for a sense of well-being in order to achieve abundance when you want to live a purpose-driven, happy, authentic life. The act of wrangling the clutter is an act of self-care of the highest order. Your things can give you a sense of security, a connection to the past and to the people you love. Your stuff tells your story. That's a good thing. However, when your things create a sense of overwhelm or chaos in your life, then it simply consumes you. And that's a bad thing.

Some people, especially creatives, live in organized chaos. They would say their stuff is not clutter. It is not perceived as clutter. They are fine; they thrive in bright color and quilt-like patterns. They are not suffering or feeling held back or blocked in any way. It creates a richness to their life, and they seem to be moving forward smoothly. I often envision a well-known photo of Karl Lagerfeld shown drawing at a desk piled so high full of cards, illustrations, papers, photos, and his cat, Choupette. Looking at it confuses me, but no one can argue with his genius. This amount of disorganized chaos is counterintuitive to being highly successful, but not in every case.

I'm referring here to those of you who get stuck in the chaos of the clutter. Physical clutter is the stuff that is figuratively consuming you.

Experts say that, on average, each US household contains around 300,000 items.[28] No wonder many of us can feel buried by our stuff.

It has been shown that there is a direct correlation between physical clutter and the negative effect it has on your physical, mental, and spiritual health: more mess, more stress!

The stress hormone cortisol has been shown to rise and fall in direct proportion to the perceived amount of clutter in one's environment.[29] Depression, poor coping skills, procrastination, and compromised social functioning can be some of the side effects.[30]

Let's consider for a moment that clutter itself is giving you clues to help you identify your unhealthy behaviors or thought patterns. It's the red flag you need to begin to eliminate your blocks, the things that are keeping you from what truly gives your life joy and meaning.

The Importance of Controlling Clutter

A recent investigation into perceptions of one's home environment examined how clutter in your home can impact your sense of well-being. The University of New Mexico's Catherine Roster and colleagues examined how clutter compromises an individual's perception of home, and ultimately one's interpretation of his or her level of life satisfaction.

The underlying premise of the study was that because many people identify so closely with their home environments, the extent to which it is cluttered can interfere with the pleasure they experience in that environment.

Roster defined "home" not simply as the physical dwelling in which you live, but more generally as "the broader constellation of experiences, meanings, and situations that shape and are actively shaped by a person in the creation of his or her lifeworld."[31]

The researchers identified a sample of adults with mild to moderate cluttering problems through The Institute for Challenging Disorganization (ICD), a nonprofit organization intended to help those who are, as you might guess, organizationally challenged. In addition to rating their own clutter-related behaviors (such as not being able to find things due to clutter), participants in the sample of nearly 1,500 adults aged 18 and older rated the extent to which they felt attached to their homes, saw their possessions as an extension of themselves, and felt that their home gave them psychological comfort.

Clutter makes it difficult to navigate through that lifeworld and to accomplish what you need to in order to live comfortably within it. For example, when your kitchen countertop is full of appliances, strewn-about mail, and random gadgets, it's going to be much more difficult to cook dinner or get that countertop looking satisfactorily clean.

I believe there is a strong correlation between home and self. Those who care about and have a strong attachment to their environment and take care of it also have a tendency to actively care for themselves. It is part of a self-care practice. Caring for the home equates with caring for self. Does your stuff contribute to or hinder your well-being?

When you have been in a space that is cluttered with stuff and is too dark or unkempt, you tend to have a visceral reaction whether you consciously recognize it or not. The clutter creates stagnant energy. The chi is unbalanced. The space does not allow for the feeling of clarity and abundance. This concept extends beyond the physical to the mental clutter in your life.

Mental Clutter

The weight and burden of physical clutter are hard enough, but it is often accompanied by mental clutter. If physical space is a reflection of your mental space, it makes sense that the physical clutter is a manifestation of something else going on that is showing up as excess stuff. In this case, there is a correlation between physical clutter and mental clutter. I do want to note that I am not a medical professional, and this book should not be referred to in place of medical help. I offer a way to look at this situation that has helped others and myself.

Mental clutter can stand on its own. Your home can be immaculate, but that does not mean you aren't suffering from mental clutter. It is the voice in your head that is not helping matters. In fact, it's making matters worse. Mental clutter consists of those thoughts that keep you stuck in the stress, overwhelm, struggle, and self-sabotaging ways of our minds, not allowing for clarity and flow. Hi, I'm Carrie, and I suffer from mental clutter!

Do you have thoughts that seemingly are on a loop constantly going around and around in your brain? It can be maddening.

Before I became a life coach and really understood what was happening, I had many thoughts, good, bad, or indifferent (but mostly bad) churning around in my brain. I could not stop it, could not shut it off, could barely slow it down. It's exhausting to have all that chatter going on in your mind, adding up to feelings of stress and anxiousness.

Some studies have shown we have between 12,000 to 60,000 thoughts a day,[32] up to 80 percent of which are negative thoughts, and many are repetitive thoughts that create restlessness or confusion within us. The Buddha defined it as the "monkey mind":

"Just as a monkey swinging through the trees grabs one branch and lets it go only to seize another, so too, that which is called thought, mind, or consciousness arises and disappears continually both day and night." [33]

The chattering of the monkey mind is a million messages that have nothing to do with stuff but keep us stuck in unhealthy behavior or thought patterns: the incessant negative self-talk destroying our confidence and instilling fear, assaulting our central nervous system with too much stimuli. On a never-ending loop, it's a beast that needs to be tamed. Will you let this little monkey win?

The Buddha encouraged his students to develop "a mind like a forest deer." [34] These gentle creatures remain alert but can quiet the distracting background noise. They can focus on the here and now, enjoying life, aware that while there might be danger at any moment, there is no danger in THIS moment. You cannot be present and be listening to your inner monologue at the same time. You must train this little monkey to behave. We must learn to coexist peacefully. Otherwise, that monkey (mind) will drive you up a tree!

This interrelationship and harmony of coexisting creatures (or microorganisms) also exist within your own body. For example, the good bacteria residing within the human digestive system have a symbiotic mutualism with humans. [35] These bacteria aid in the digestion of organic compounds necessary for sustenance. They also produce vitamins and hormone-like compounds and are important for a healthy immune system. Having a healthy gut leads to having a healthy body, which leads to having a healthy mind, which leads to having a healthy attitude, and so on and so on.

Your mental and physical health requires your brain to practice this same kind of mutualism, and in this scenario, clutter is the enemy. When clutter exists, your brain signals there is a problem—you feel unsettled, confined, even physically sluggish. You need to look at these feelings as a sign alerting you to a problem in your environment: physical, emotional, spiritual, or spatial.

By removing clutter, you can employ coping skills that will shift you from fear, anxiety, and worry into joy, love, and inner peace.

The following exercises can help you quiet the "monkey mind" within.

1. Journal your thoughts: anything that comes up when your monkey mind is chattering away. Fears, regrets, struggles, self-doubt, tasks, anything that the monkey on your back is blasting at you. Seeing the words on paper helps to take the power out of thoughts that create suffering; it will also help you see patterns that you can now address in a healthier way than letting them ruminate in the recesses of your mind.

2. Engage all your senses to stop the negative talk in its tracks. Pay full attention to where you are in the moment: What are you seeing, smelling, hearing? Who are you with? How do you feel in your body? Go inward and let your body give your mind a rest. When you are paying attention to the "here and now," you are not in your mind.

3. Do any activity that quiets the mind, such as exercising, playing golf, coloring, creating, reading, or organizing. This is exactly why meditation is often prescribed; it is the perfect way to gain peace and learn to shut out the noise that takes up a lot of headspace. The point is to override your negative internal dialog by doing something that requires

all your attention. You can only focus on one thing: change the thing you are focusing on to get out of your head and into the present moment.

There is so much power in the words we use. Take the power out of the negative thoughts you have on repeat and instead repeat "I am at peace with _____" (a situation, a thought, a decision, something out of our control) over and over and over until you believe it.

4. Talk to a trusted friend or therapist, or life coach about your thoughts. Do not repress your feelings. Respect them; they will come out in subtle, destructive ways if you don't. Having someone there as a sounding board may help you identify patterns that come up over and over that you have trouble seeing by yourself. I also find that saying things out loud gives them a different tone and can help you change the narrative.

5. Breathe, not the ordinary breathing that you do without thinking, but mindful deep, diaphragmatic breathing. Choose what feels comfortable for you; any breathing technique has the power to bring you back to the present. The important thing is to think about each breath as you slowly inhale air and exhale toxic thoughts.

Mental Clutter Hangs Out in the Closet

A client I keep in touch with goes through her closet every chance she gets. Every time I call, she is "in her closet." I think, is there ever an end? The answer is emphatically "no" because, metaphorically speaking, she is shifting her emotional baggage around to avoid solving the deeper issues that are hidden in her closet-cleanout behavior.

She will never get through the "closet cleanout" because she is not willing to change the thoughts that keep undermining her behavior.

Boxes, bags, hangers, and random remnants—physical representations of skeletons—symbolize her inability to change her circumstances and thereby grow into the more than capable woman she is. Her inability to move forward will keep her closet shifting forever. There is always a closet to tackle, and she must be at the ready.

I give her credit for getting in there and having the desire to do the work. She feels like she is taking action because she is physically moving things around, but the emotional clutter hiding in plain sight keeps the goal at bay. Unresolved emotional trauma shows up in a myriad of ways.

The closet is a hotbed for issues to hang out in. I often discover my clients' limiting beliefs just by going through their closets.

People often keep items they just can't part with because they hold a certain memory, whether it is a bohemian sundress they wore when they went on their first date with their husband or a power suit reminding them of the corporate job they left years before or a crop top that should no longer see the light of day. These items may be nostalgic but what they really say is: I am not representing where my life is presently. I am not accepting myself right here, right now. I am holding on to baggage, unable to let go.

Clothes hold energy and have imprinted memories on them. They have the power to take you back to a time and a place, like a song from your high school days. Your life in clothes—keep the memory, put the physical representation of it away. Say goodbye, *adieu*.
Could there be some fear involved? Fear of moving forward? Fear of change? Fear of success? Fear is a powerful deterrent. Better the devil you know than the devil you don't. I ask, "What is on the other side

of fear?"

Your closet should be an immaculate representation of your lifestyle right now or what you aspire to do.

This might be a good time to go into your closet and take a good hard look at the contents—are there "limiting beliefs" lurking within? Ask the following questions about each item; you might find some unexpected answers.

- How does this article of clothing make me feel?
- Does this article of clothing represent something that makes me feel good or bad?
- How well does it fit?
- Is it a true reflection of who I am?
- Do I feel like I look my best in it?
- Do I love myself in it?
- When was the last time I wore it?
- Do I attach a person, place, or thing to it?
- Does it represent my life in the now?
- Can I step into this as my most authentic self in the future?

If the answer to any of these questions is more negative than positive—purge it.

We all know how to declutter, but sometimes we just don't do it. Like we all know how to diet, but our psyche gets in our way. I am always interested in getting to the root cause of a behavior: it can show you something about yourself, maybe an area in your life that you could work on.

If, metaphorically, your closet was a vessel for your soul, what would you allow in?

The How and the Why

The How without the Why does not answer the question, how did I get here? The unwanted behavior will rear its ugly head again in time if you do not address the root cause. This is a general life hack that extends far beyond your closet.

You must want to make a change. You cannot do the same thing over and over and expect a different result. You actually have to take a new action. Taking action can be really scary. Taking one baby step toward your result and seeing how that feels may encourage you to take another baby step, then another. You are rewiring your brain. You are changing your reality. You are walking into a new future.

If you hate to throw something out and just can't bear to part with it, store it in a keepsake box because it holds a happy memory and maybe revisit it at a later date.

This should be your mantra: donate, purge, relocate, repurpose—repeat.

Closet as a Gateway for Manifestation

I recently worked with a lovely woman who was newly divorced. She had just bought a new apartment, and we talked about how to design not only this small apartment bathed in light but also her new life. She understood the role she played in causing the dissolution of her marriage, appropriately mourned the loss, and felt she was ready to step into her future: from challenge comes growth.

She was a little apprehensive but excited at the prospect of starting to date again. We talked about who she wanted to attract, what she wanted her future relationships to look like, and where she hoped to go on dates. We happened to be standing in her closet as we had the dating conversation.

I stood in a cavernous, empty, but well-appointed walk-in and asked, "Where are all your clothes?"

"Oh, I left everything behind. My old clothes were part of my old life. I want a new life." "Dress for that," I said.

She filled her closet with a few cute, age-appropriate dresses, perfect for date nights, some sportswear for the active lifestyle she continues to enjoy. She even purchased casual travel outfits to have at the ready in case she got whisked off at a moment's notice.

You have to set an intention and then set yourself up for success and avoid roadblocks. If someone invited this woman away, she might say, "Oh, I have nothing to wear." Not anymore. She was prepared with a current passport, beachwear, skiwear, and luggage. These are things she wants to continue to do with a companion. Chances are, if she is ready to go, the man she calls forth will be ready to take her, or she'll take him.

This scenario is the first step toward behaving "as if," which is the cornerstone of manifesting.

The bedroom was sunny and optimistic-looking. The artwork included pairs of things. She bought rose quartz and put it on the night tables because it promotes harmony in relationships and brings with it the energy of love, trust, and compassion. I made sure there were no remnants of past relationships lurking in the shadows. She was free and clear to move forward. We covered all the bases. When you practice awareness, have clarity, and know your goals, you can begin to call in what you want. This client had done the inner work, and now she was ready to call to action that which she desired. Just reading this, don't you feel hopeful for her?

If you keep taking action as your future self, clearing closets as your future self, holding yourself up as your future self, living "as if" you are your future self, then you can manifest all kinds of things.

The awareness behind our thoughts and actions allows us to let go of the emotions keeping us in resistance. Removing resistance allows for flow. Flow creates the ability to spring forward and in the forward movement is growth.

There's no right or wrong, good or bad. Whether you want inner happiness, more money, or that dream job, each desire is valid and requires the same amount of action—and letting go.

The letting go was always the hardest part for me. When we want something, we tend to hold tighter. It feels counterintuitive to let go of the person, place, or thing we desire. We become laser-focused on getting "it." This is fear. Your ego is speaking, and you must not listen. We must become unattached to the outcome. Like a feather in the wind, notice it floating by, just notice. You might comment, "Oh look, what a beautiful feather is floating by," and then it's gone, swept away on the undulating breeze. You see it, you enjoy it for what it is in the moment, and the moment is gone.

Universally, the basic definition of the Law of Attraction states that energy is attracted to similar energy.[36] This can either help you or harm you, depending on what energy you put out.

Your life reflects back what you put out. Your challenges may be real, but that doesn't mean you have to focus on them. If you choose to focus on what is good and what is right, what you are grateful for, and what is working, you are creating the potential to make a change in your life. You are shifting to allow thoughts of gratitude and optimism to fill you up.

Mike Dooley, *New York Times* best-selling author and the man who coined the phrase "thoughts become things," uses an analogy that I love. In his popular program outlined in *Playing the Matrix*, he expounds on the notion of defining what you want in general terms, beginning with the end result and working backward.[37] We need to be open to any possibility or opportunity. He describes this in terms we can all understand: picture yourself setting your GPS on your desired destination (your goal). You know *where* you want to end up, but at any given moment, your GPS might change course to get you there faster, more safely, using less gas, or with more ease. If you were to follow your GPS as it takes you around obstacles or off toll roads, you would get to where you were going by staying open to any and all possibilities, even those you might not have foreseen.

There may be a roundabout way to get to where you're going, but if you are set on the one route you are familiar with and are not open to other possibilities, you may miss an opportunity that comes your way simply by not seeing it. Always stay focused on the big picture but unattached to the details of how you are going to get there.

For example, to set the intention "I desire a vacation home next year" is a good general jumping-off point. To say, "I desire a beach house in Montauk" is very specific. The goal really is to own a beach house, ideally in Montauk but let's be open to see what happens. Set your intention and go about educating yourself about what you need in order to buy a beach house. Do you have the savings, or do you need a mortgage? Will you hire a broker or house-hunt on your own?

You begin taking action steps toward making that beach house happen—checking the MLS listings, driving through neighborhoods around your desired area in Montauk, dreaming of the lazy, hazy summer days spent lying on the beach. Imagine what it would feel like to be at your house, sitting on the porch, watching the sunset on a perfect summer day with the last warm rays obscuring your view as the sun slips into the water. Visualize the details. Smell the salty air, feel the humidity on your skin as you swing from your hanging lounge chair on the front porch.

Meanwhile, you are still living your life, going to work, enjoying your Saturday nights out while fantasizing about the beach house but trusting the process and letting go. Your desire was to own that home in Montauk but suddenly and unexpectedly, your aunt passes away, and you inherit an old home in Asbury Park, a block from the beach. Asbury Park is not Montauk, but *Money* magazine named it the second-best beach town in the US behind Pompano Beach, Florida. The eclectic vibe there attracts a diverse group of interesting people doing interesting things that ignites your curiosity.

All things considered, this is a perfect destination that might not have been on your radar but seems a great spot. However, you could also sell the property and buy a small place in Montauk. You now have a choice among beach houses. How could this have happened?

You asked, the universe answered. This must have happened for a reason. You believed it into being. This is what can happen when you set an intention, take actionable steps forward, and keep the details vague. Be end-result oriented, but do not attach to the end result. This is manifestation.

Define what you want. Be clear in your intention, but be open to how you might receive it or what form it might appear in. Then act "as if" you had already received it (in practical terms).

I love this idea so much because manifestation is not about the goal itself (not exactly); it's about the feeling that you imagine achieving it will bring you. You are benefiting in the present by feeling the joy you believe it will bring you in the future. It is a perfect practice for those who like immediate gratification.

Clearing away the physical and mental clutter in your life is essential for opening up energy and clearing a path to allow for abundance in your home—but that's only a part of the equation. The thoughts in your head, the negative self-talk, the drama-filled friendships, any mental clutter that takes up bandwidth in your brain has to be acknowledged and dissolved in order for calm to come over you. In time, you will become your future. So, it's not about getting this, that, or the other thing. It's about who you become in the process of *becoming* your future. So, go be your future self!

TAKEAWAYS

- Clutter, physical and mental, is enemy No. 1.

- Understand your attachment to things: people, places, or objects. How do they serve you?

- Clutter is directly correlated to stress.

- Getting to the root cause of an issue is the only way to ensure that you will solve the issue.

- Awareness allows you to move out of resistance.

- The law of attraction requires a certain amount of attachment and release.

5

AWARENESS FOR THE WIN

Awareness is like the sun. When it shines on
things, they are transformed.
—Thich Nhat Hanh

I ONCE HAD A REPUTATION FOR BEING ANNOYED all the time. Everything annoyed me: traffic, bad customer service, my work, being in a noisy restaurant, rude people, anything that did not make sense to me. You see the problem.

Someone joked I should get a Pennsylvania license plate that read "IM ANOYD." It's funny, but the truth is often hidden in humor. This was not who I wanted to be, what I wanted others to think of me, or what I wanted my children to replicate. What kind of role model was I presenting, especially when I was driving and exhibiting signs of road rage? "People are so oblivious and thoughtless," I'd tell myself whenever I fell back into the old thinking pattern. It was a constant push and pull.

I was envious of the easygoing guy or gal sitting behind the wheel, listening to the radio, maybe singing along, as if they had nowhere to be, nothing on their mind, and were out for a leisurely Sunday ride. I wanted to look like that, hair blowing in the wind, smile on my face, feeling easy breezy—but no. I was the woman hugging her chest from anxiety with a look of scorn on her face, possibly giving you the finger as I passed you.

Stress, negativity, fear, and anger do funny things to people and, by their very nature, make us uncomfortable. Something had to change; of course, the answer was obvious. It was up to me, damn it! If I wanted to feel better, I had to change. When you know better, you can do better!

The greatest agent for change is self-awareness. From there, you can begin to paint a different picture or tell a different story to release those influences that create suffering. You can begin to evaluate your current state of consciousness by first asking yourself: Am I reducing stress? Am I exercising and eating right? Do I love the work I do? Do I enjoy the relationships in which I engage? Is my home environment supportive of my higher self?

My Home Is Chaotic

One of my first and best examples of how our mind and our home so similarly coexist is a story about a design client I was working with soon after I became a certified life coach. I walked through her home, and we got to know each other while deciding where to begin and what her family's priorities were.

We stopped in the playroom, which was a den in a past life, just off the kitchen. There was a mock stage, costumes, and props everywhere. Being the mother of boys, I am unfamiliar with the accoutrements of little girls and the imaginary lives they lead, but I certainly understand the power of play. There was an arts and crafts corner, a futon for catching up on all things "tween" on TV, along with the requisite dolls, building blocks, and board games.

The mom was expressing her frustration at her lack of ability to keep the room neat and her desire to design a more efficient space. We moved from there to the living room, then up the stairs and into the master bedroom, and all the while,she casually talked about what she had done in her past and what she was hoping to accomplish in the near future, as she was anxious to get back to work. With her youngest ready to start school full-time, she was interested in learning software code to further her business offerings, bring mindfulness into public schools through some type of program, and possibly write a book. All big ideas.

I said, "Your mind sounds like the playroom looks."

It stopped her mid-sentence. She thought about it a minute and immediately understood what I meant. That was where we began. I gave her the assignment of going through the playroom, organizing the costumes, keeping what fit, getting rid of what did not. She corralled similar toys and their parts, categorized art supplies, and contained each in its own drawer in a chest we bought, all the while sifting through the thoughts in her head about what feels right, right now, regarding her next career move.

I told her to go inward. Did anything feel more urgent or light her up more when she thought about doing it? Could she let go of anything? Could she make a short-term plan and a long-term plan? There was plenty of time to do everything, just not at the same time. Our minds, like our living spaces, cannot handle too many tasks and handle them well.

A wall of built-ins that included desks that could be raised for growing children was the jumping-off point for this client. We took out the TV; the room became a play-and-work-only zone. Everything had a place, and everything in the playroom was being used and taken care of. It was a teaching moment for her children because she and her husband had taught them to respect their belongings and put them away, while it was also an opportunity for mom to clarify what her next step might be.

The clarity of how the room functioned mirrored the clarity she found to make an intelligent decision about moving her career forward. As she was organizing the playroom, before we began installing the custom shelving system, she decided that bringing mindfulness into the schools might be better left to someone else. That is a tall task. Learning code and doing something with that was a definite maybe but would take time. Writing a local history book was already in her wheelhouse, so that seemed like the logical place to start. So, she did.

With the book published and checked off her to-do list, she was free to move on and learn code and is now an entrepreneur helping small businesses achieve visibility and success.

The playroom is kept tidy not only because of our organizational efforts but because everyone senses that mommy is happier, and when mommy is happy, peace reigns over the land. This is a beautiful success story. You are never done with the process, though. It is a lifetime of prioritizing, questioning, and purging. The goal is to surround yourself with the things you love or deem to be useful or necessary.

How does developing awareness apply to your home?

There are three things you should naturally extend to your home itself: being aware of what is truly important to you, what you value, and the principles you live by. Your home is ideally an extension of you, your thoughts, dreams, goals, and priorities.

Interior design can be thought of as visual storytelling. You want to tell a compelling story with you as the protagonist. The narrative is what you have chosen to put in your home, including elements such as cleanliness, sights, sounds, and smells, and how each piece of furniture, as well as the artwork and books you display, all coexist with the others in a way that allows visitors to receive a sense of who you are. They see you because you have told them—visually. Your space becomes more dimensional with the more awareness you possess; the more your environment has the ability to fulfill you, the richer the story you tell.

Your living space will reward you by making you feel like you are getting a big, warm hug at the end of a hectic day. It is a symbiotic relationship: you treat yourself and your home with respect, with love, with cleanliness, and your home will reward you in kind. It becomes a place where your well-being takes top billing. You are then not only allowing yourself to be "seen" by others, but you are taking charge of your health. Why? Because coming home to a place you love reduces your cortisol levels, reduces anxiety and stress, and allows you to rest and recharge. It is a matter of integrity in design and in life.

All of these factors determine your level of fulfillment. You are the writer of the story of your own destiny. You get to choose how your autobiography unfolds, page by page. You determine if you are the heroine who succeeds at life or the damsel in distress. You can be the king or queen of your kingdom—or you can be the peasant plowing the fields. You could live in misery or happily ever after. It's all up to you. The things that happen to you, the experiences you have in life create your emotions. Your emotions are the byproduct of the stories you tell yourself. To go from dark comedy to rom/com only requires a shift in perspective.

It sounds amazing when you think of it that way, doesn't it? It feels as if you're in command; you have the control—because you are, and you do. To have the ability to be observant and have awareness is to be present; to be present is to be mindful. This is your first building block.

I was at a party many years ago where the hosts brought in a psychic to do readings. I don't know if I exactly believe in psychics, but they're fun to hear nonetheless. I am always just so curious and hopeful one will tell me something exciting—perhaps that I'll have my Tudor or contemporary dream home one day. Perhaps the psychic will say, "The weight you are carrying will drop off you, and your clothes will look amazing on your new, svelte figure. Your children will be blessed with happy, successful lives, and you will have amazing grandchildren."

When it was my turn, I was thinking pragmatically and asked, "Will I be happy, and will I live a long, healthy life?"

She paused for a moment. My heart began to pound as she took my hand and said,

"You will have everything you need."

For many years after, I would recall the moment and think the same thing, "What kind of answer was that?" Now I realize the brilliance of it. *I will have everything I need.* Non-believers will tell you that psychics give blanket statements that apply to everyone, so when something happens, because you live life and constant change is certain, you can look back and say, "Aha, that psychic was right."

I did get what I asked for. The phrase, "you will have everything you need," has depth and intellect if the subject (me) chooses to hear it in a more profound way.

My beliefs or my thoughts become my reality. If I believe I will have everything I need—so it shall be. Therefore, I have everything I need. The psychic was right. I am safe, I have food, I have shelter, I am loved, my body has not totally shut down. I have friends and family that lift me up. How lucky am I? I have it all! I am blessed. I am abundant! Can you have it all? Is such a thing even possible? For me now, through this journey, I know it is possible to have it all because I have everything I need. If you possess self-awareness, have a practice of gratitude, and a strong belief in your own self-worth, you too can ride the waves of life's ebb and flow, always coming out on top.

Some develop awareness quite naturally as they mature; some need to practice it every day until it becomes second nature. The best way to develop better self-awareness is through stillness. When you silence all the noise within and around you, you begin to hear your soul's desire. Ask yourself these four soul questions:

> Who am I at my core?
> What do I really, truly want?
> What am I grateful for?
> What is my purpose in life?

It doesn't matter if you have an answer right away or not. Just keep asking the questions.

The beautiful thing is, awareness can be learned and cultivated. It is a daily practice that only enriches your life. You can learn how to steer toward your North Star, that which makes you happy and feels best, ultimately leading you to your authentic self.

For many people, reaching a level of self-awareness is difficult because they allow themselves to be controlled by their primitive selves.

Your Lizard Brain

"Be fearful, resist, go slow, stay small," that's the lizard or reptilian brain talking.[38] It has good intentions, but it holds you back. It is the most primitive part of your brain. That part of your brain is known to go into fight or flight mode at the drop of a hat. It is the little voice that convinces you that you can't be, can't do, or can't have something. When activated, it can be brutal. It wants nothing more than to keep you from doing anything new or risky, or uncomfortable. The lizard brain doesn't like change. It thinks it is protecting you, but by planting ideas in your head that keep you from trying new things, appearing vulnerable, or taking a leap in life, it shuts you down.

This "self-protective" belief is created in what we call one of a pair of almond-shaped clusters in your brain: the *amygdala*. The amygdala is the primitive lack-and-attack attitude we carry within.[39]

It is a part of the subconscious. It pushes you into fight or flight mode at the first sign of a threat. It allows you to process a threat and react quickly, say, in the case of a saber tooth tiger hunting you. We humans grew and evolved, but the reptilian part of our brain, a remainder of our cave ancestor's brain, did not. Interestingly, the threat we perceive is often not reality. It is of our mind's own making.

Author, educator, entrepreneur Seth Godin said, "The lizard brain is hungry, scared, angry, and horny."[40]

Nothing too complex there. The lizard brain takes care of basic needs and is that voice in your head that says, "Don't do that." "Be careful, you might get hurt." "What are you thinking?" "I'm not good enough." "My boss hates me." And a million other messages that do not serve you well.

The lizard brain is your ego, it's fear-based, and it enjoys conflict and can be aggressive. It uses past thoughts and future "what ifs" to try and take you down. You can't get rid of it, but you can learn to coexist with it, often peacefully after you wrestle it into submission. More often than not, you are completely unaware that these "limiting beliefs" are looming just below the surface, quietly waiting in silence, biding their time to jump up and sting you with biting words or thoughts in an effort to get you to change your behavior. The ego has the power to raise you up or knock you down.

By understanding where these thoughts come from, you can train yourself to not allow this thinking to infiltrate your life, your relationships, or your body. Understand that you have the power within to change the narrative. You must recognize this voice and disempower it, or it will lead you astray.

When working with my life-coaching clients, I often use the following visualization exercise as a great tool for helping to strengthen positive thoughts and eviscerate negative ones.

Begin by trying to visualize your "inner lizard." Really see it. "It" can be anything or anyone, made up or real. Then literally draw a picture of it, in all its disturbing detail, and finally, name it. My inner lizard's name is *Jokey* because she's not to be taken seriously. (Inner lizard / naming your lizard, adapted from the work of Martha Beck. The concept is written about in her book *Steering by Starlight*.[41])

Whenever I feel threatened for no obvious reason, my anxiety begins to rise. When I'm overanalyzing, overreacting, or overdramatizing a story in my mind and I begin to feel triggered, I say to myself,

"Stop, that's just Jokey messing with me." Jokey is a joke, just like the story I am telling myself and believing. It immediately mitigates the power of the thought. You recognized it, said, "Stop it," said, "Thank you very much, I hear you, but I am choosing to ignore you and to move on."

You can do some real damage to your mental health if you allow destructive thoughts to rule you. You can see how damaging your reptilian brain can be if you don't keep it in check. Like a reptile sheds its skin, you can shed the limiting beliefs of the ego that do not serve you and keep you in a state of small-mindedness. The reptilian brain doesn't seem to want us to be healthy, wealthy, and wise. Your brain, in fact, does not tell us the whole truth when it comes to being healthy, wealthy, and wise—but your body does.

It's all about learning to listen to yourself, to go within. This requires you to become still. You cannot explore the depth of your being if you are surrounded by a cacophony of sights, sounds, and stimuli.

Begin by tuning back into your body. You have it within yourself to employ this practice. Give yourself the gift of stillness, creating space in your mind to reach a place of inner peace and deeper happiness.

To be still allows for that space to open up, to breathe, to observe, to not react when that is your first inclination. Stepping back takes discipline and patience. You can do this when you recognize that you are not your thoughts and that feeling good is your goal.

When a thought arises that's unhealthy or creates a certain amount of suffering:

- Stop.

- Observe the thought.

- Name it as your inner lizard—your ego.

- Recognize that you can change it.

Then, each time you hear that self-sabotaging voice in your head, notice it and tell yourself that it's just (your inner lizard's name) messing with you. It is not true.

Repeat after me—I have the power to replace:

> **I can't** with **I can!**
> **I won't** with **I will!**
> **I'm afraid** with **I must!**

Turn any negative "I" statement into a positive one.

The ability to skillfully uncover unhealthy patterns of behavior about yourself, others, or the world around you—often unconsciously—through thought or deed has the power to be helpful or harmful. Helpful because you can think about it as an invitation to examine what is coming up for you. You can look at these thoughts as messages—messages that you need to dig into and sort out. It is a beautiful opportunity for self-investigation.

But it can also be harmful if you don't recognize and practice self-awareness. Without it, you will keep making the same mistakes, living as a victim or arguing with reality, living unhappily with the things you desire just out of reach and never really knowing why.

The goal is to always be aware of what you need for your mind, body, spirit, and living space so you can give it to yourself. You can heal yourself. No one else will. Your mind lies to you, like that little lizard that wants to sabotage and derail you. When you go within, learn to be still, listen to your inner voice, you'll get to know yourself better. You will recognize the cues to help stop the madness that overwhelms you. Seemingly small changes lead you in a more positive direction and set off neurons in the brain. When these neurons peak, they create energy for a high positive response, which in turn will set off a neural network that elicits behavior to continue on this path of pleasure-seeking or high positive rewards.[42]

This will make such a difference in your day-to-day life on the journey toward your best life.

Limiting beliefs keep you playing small, keep you fearful, keep you in negative, self-sabotaging patterns. The not-so-funny thing is, you often don't realize you have these beliefs. How are you supposed to identify them if you can't see them?

How to Identify Your Limiting Beliefs

- Ask trusted friends and family; it is always easier to spot something in someone else than in yourself. Take a random poll.

- Be open to really hearing about others' perceptions of you.

- If you spot it, you got it. When you have uncomfortable feelings toward another, it is often a trigger about something you are feeling within yourself. View it as an invitation to look inward and examine why these feelings are coming up.

- Do you feel stuck in an area? What are the stories you tell yourself to support the feeling of being stuck? If you focus on "stuckness," you will be given more "stuckness." You need to turn your thoughts around and tell a different story.

- Are you suffering in an area of your life? Suffering is optional. There is always a way out.

- Can you identify patterns of thought or behavior that are not serving you? Changing self-sabotaging thoughts or behavior patterns is the basis for transformation.

- List what you think is working. Then list what you don't think works for you. Tune back into your body.

We all have it within us to employ this practice. You are creating space in your mind in an effort to reach a place of inner peace and deeper happiness. To be still allows for space to open up—space to breath, to observe, to not react when that is your first inclination. Stepping back into stillness takes discipline and patience.

Becoming Stress-less

You may live in a state of chronic stress. Most of us do this without realizing it's not meant to be a normal state or, worse yet, that there is no alternative. You almost assume you must live in this tumultuousness if you work at a job, have children at home, or live on this planet. Thinking that it is your career, family, relationships, or lifestyle that is causing us the stress is seeing the situation from the wrong perspective.

You can certainly change your circumstances, and this may help, but, invariably, it is your perspective that needs to change. Physical and emotional health is about balance and harmony. An out-of-balance energy system stresses the body. What causes stress? The answer is really quite simple. Negative emotions, feelings, thoughts, ideas, and beliefs cause stress. Every thought and emotion has a physiologic response. If you are suffering, you are in a stressful state.

Chronic stress on the body shows up in myriad ways, none good. Stress comes from anywhere and sometimes out of the blue. That long commute, the kids misbehaving, a sick parent, feeling isolated, a fight with a friend or spouse, lack of sleep, social media. Small daily things add up and adversely affect your health on a cellular level. Before you know it, you're short of breath, your pulse rises, your cortisol levels shoot up, your cognitive ability goes down, your autoimmune system is compromised, you gain weight, you look older. Holy moly: stop the ride, I want to get off.[43]

On the American Institute of Stress website, there is a list of 50 signs and symptoms of stress.[44] Managing negative emotions requires us to get in touch with our feelings. It allows us to question what is coming up for us. We determine why we are feeling what we are feeling; what is the trigger?

If it's left unchecked and you experience chronic stress on a regular basis, your physical and emotional health suffers. If your methods of coping with stress aren't contributing to your greater emotional and physical health, it's time to find healthier coping mechanisms. There are many healthy ways to manage and cope with stress, but they all require behavioral change. Having the clarity to recognize the need for change creates the confidence to keep you moving in forward motion. You can either change the situation or change your reaction. Just noticing and becoming aware allows a little room for something to shift.

Developing self-awareness allows you to spot the anxiety, depression, abusive behavior, overwhelm, people-pleasing, narcissism, stress, etc., that you might otherwise not be aware of.

Using my earlier road rage story as an example, when I now start thinking that everyone is oblivious and thoughtless, I can say, "That's my old story about drivers." I can control my lizard brain, there's Jokey again rearing her ugly head, and I can create a different story. It's one that feels better and makes me, if not happier, at least more at peace. I am going to enjoy these moments in the car listening to and singing along with the radio. This is my time, my special time. I think—oh, this song takes me back to a happy memory from college. Look, there's a beautiful rainbow in front of me. I am so in awe of Mother Nature for having created such beauty after the rain—I choose to enjoy it. I will get to where I am going and be in a better frame of mind. I change the thought pattern to anything more pleasant than the thought that creates suffering.

I am choosing to stop the negative emotions that I am creating with my beliefs, changing the energy within me and around me. By mastering this technique, you too can clear the negative clutter in your mind because your thoughts create your reality. Your energy shifts from that of a cloudy day to that of a more beautiful rainbow high in the sky. Would you rather be a gray cloud or a rainbow?

I was talking to a friend who was telling me of her harrowing experience shopping around the holidays. The mall at Christmas is one of my worst nightmares. I avoid it at all costs. She, on the other hand, is a Black Friday shopper. Carpe diem, if you are going to do that to yourself, you better enjoy the experience. As she was telling me about the crowds and the shoving and the stress, the inexperienced employees, and the long lines, I could feel her energy shift from that of my pleasant lunch partner to an anxious cohort.

"Then why do you do that to yourself?" I asked.

"I used to do it with my mother and aunt. I have such wonderful memories of the craziness and laughter. It was a big part of my childhood. We always had so much fun spending the day together. I enlisted my daughters when they were old enough, and that became our tradition as well. Now my mother has passed, and my girls are grown. The fun is gone. I felt obligated to keep up the tradition, so I enlisted a few girlfriends, but it's not the same," she explained.

The beautiful memories will always be with my friend. Those are to be cherished. But things change, and we may need to pivot occasionally to remain moving in the direction that brings us joy.

If it doesn't serve you, let it go. Say it again—out loud.

Tried and True Stress Relievers

1. Exercise.

2. Keep a journal and jot down each time you feel stressed or upset. Journaling turns chaos into order, unconscious to conscious on the page.

    a. See if you can identify the trigger.

    b. What was happening right before you felt triggered?

    c. What story are you telling yourself right now?

    d. Where in your body do you feel it, how does it manifest?

    e. What did you do in reaction to the stress? Was it helpful or harmful? If harmful, what could you have done differently, with clarity, to turn the outcome around?

3. Create a pro, con, and neutral list.

    a. Write down anything, and everything you can think of that is impeding your joy. Under each heading, ask: is this harming me, helping me, or am I neutral? Do I feel tired, underwhelmed, or have a sense of obligation when I engage with this person, place, or thing? List as much as possible. You will begin to see what you might need to step away from or what behaviors need to be altered.

Each of these steps requires you to think about things intellectually, then consider how it makes you feel emotionally.

Connecting to Your Body

Have you ever given any thought to whether you feel connected to your body? Do you think of yourself as having a strong mind/ body connection? I am referring to how the brain, your thoughts, and your emotions interact and how they influence your body's function. Your body is like a beautiful, omnipotent heart map. It holds all the wisdom and divine knowledge you need to keep yourself balanced in a state of peace and harmony.

You want to keep the channels of your mind/body connection open, aligned, and communicating as one. When you do, you are vibrating higher, and energy can flow through you with ease. When you are vibrating higher and energy-blocks dissipate, abundance is free to flow. Inner turmoil becomes inner harmony. Dissatisfaction becomes satisfaction. Resistance becomes acceptance.

I always fancied myself as having a very strong mind/body connection. I intuitively knew it, but until I learned the following exercise, I was not living as joyfully as I could have been or as I am now. What I do now is to go inward and ask my body how it feels—then I follow through accordingly.

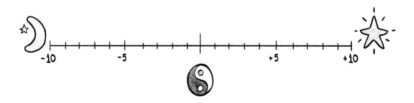

First, picture a horizontal line, the center being zero. This zero represents your neutral state. To the left, moving from 0 to -10 at the furthest point, in between -1, -2, -3, -4, through -9, and stopping at -10 represents unpleasant to painful feelings going from bad to the worst feeling something can provoke, that's your negative meter. This tool is modeled after the *Body Compass* taught in *Wayfinder Life Coach Training* by Martha Beck.[45]

Close your eyes and picture the horizontal line as your "meter" in your mind's eye. Think about a time when you felt very unhappy or had a painful experience. Notice what is going on physically in your body as you recall this unpleasant memory. Are your palms sweaty? Does your chest feel tight? Perhaps your eyes are welling up as you remember this most unpleasant memory.

Second, ask yourself where on the negative side of this "meter" might that experience fall? Your goal is to associate a physical feeling with the number where it registers on your imaginary mind/body compass. Your goal going forward is to steer clear of the negative side of the mind/body compass when possible. If you can't steer clear of things that put your body in a state of discomfort, ask yourself what you can do to take an experience that would have registered at, say, a -7 up to, say, a -2? Negative 2 will feel better than a negative 7, right? You can alleviate some of the displeasure. You really want to limit any activity that provokes negative feelings or lessen them whenever possible.

Third, shake off the negativity. Do as Taylor Swift does and shake it off. Literally, shake your body to release the energy of the negative memory.

Fourth, close your eyes again. Do the same exercise but think of a really happy, joyful experience. Picture yourself in that image, notice how your body is reacting to the sheer pleasure of the memory. Did a smile appear on your face? Did your heart race while reminiscing? Envisioning your joy meter going from the neutral 0 upward through the positive side of the scale with +1 being small joys to +10 being the most joyful you have ever felt—your goal always is to try to stay on the positive side of the meter.

I go inward, and while I am asking myself how this makes me feel, I am scanning my body, continuously visualizing where on the meter my feelings fall and how any given event, space, person, or experience makes me feel. Obviously, your goal is always to ask, "Where do I fall on the meter? How does (fill in the blank) make me feel?"

I look inward to my body's response to everything. Every decision I make, I ask: How does this make me FEEL? Where does it fall on the mind/body compass?

That also goes for every question: Do I want fish or meat for dinner? Do I want to paint my bedroom blue or green? How would this make me feel? Do I want to go on a weekend getaway with my children or leave them with a sitter? Would driving or flying make me more comfortable?

You can literally close your eyes and scan any question through your mind/body compass, visualizing where your feelings fall on the meter. Just ask yourself, "How does this make me feel?"

I love this tool because It asks you to go inward. It forces you to get in touch with your body. It helps make every experience the best it can be.

- Will flowers make me happier? YES.

- Will a bath make me feel good? YES.

- Do I need to go to that business dinner my husband would like me to attend? NO.

- Would going out with that couple who always think they're better than us make me happy? Hell, NO.

- I have to go to "back to school night," but I don't have to sit with the catty woman in my son's class.

- I enjoy sitting in my backyard but would love a little more privacy. What will make me feel like I have more privacy, a fence or hedges?

You get the idea. This is not a conversation about *having* to do things. It is a conversation about *choosing* to do things in your best interest or making an experience the best it can be. Life is too short to be unhappy!

Of course, we all have to do things we don't want to do, like get a root canal, or go to the annual business conference. But ask yourself, "What can I do to make it more pleasurable?" For example, can I eat ice cream and watch my favorite movie after the root canal? Can I reach out to a long-lost friend living in the city where the conference is located?

Now that you've taken the thing that might have been a nuisance and made it a little more tolerable by attaching something positive to it. Focus on that.

Your newfound awareness helps you get past the times you must muddle through. Realize that this too shall pass: *I can take back some control.* Having some control helps you feel powerful: *I will gain my freedom, and nobody can take away my happiness.* On the path to optimal health, joy and pleasure are pavers. With self-awareness, you become aware of possibility and see things in new and different ways.

Keep It Going

Awareness, or the practice of mindfulness, is like a muscle you have to exercise. Living a mindful life awakens your emotional, physical, and spiritual self. It ebbs and flows throughout the day but resides in the present moment.

1. *Meditate.* Meditation (the art of introspection) is optimal for developing mindfulness. It requires an inner state of stillness. When your mind is clear and quieted, you are not focused on the world around you. Having said that, there are so many avenues for exploring introspection. It is a little like trying on clothes. You might have to "try on" several meditation practices before you find one that resonates with you. If at first, you don't succeed try, try again. There is no right way to meditate. There's your way.

2. *Write in a journal.* Julia Cameron, author of *The Artist's Way,* encourages morning pages, where you just free-write longhand for three pages every morning.[46] There must be something to this. We're still talking about *The Artist's Way,* and the book was written almost 30 years ago. You use a stream of consciousness writing and see what comes up. Don't

worry about grammar, spelling, or sentence structure—just write. The thought is that you will see themes come up, find clarity in situations, or possibly solve a problem.

Freewriting, or reflective journaling, allows the less disciplined person the opportunity to articulate hopes, dreams, and clarity of thought. As an added benefit, you are left with a record of your progress when you look back. You are able to see how far you've come, which is helpful when you feel as though you haven't made progress. Journaling, along with the benefit of reflection, allows for greater awareness.

3. *Try active breathwork.* Breathwork is one of the most overlooked stress reducers and one of the greatest agents of change. It helps to channel the physical or emotional effects of stress into a healthier coping mechanism.

    Breathe in slowly and deeply. Keep the tip of your tongue glued lightly to the back of your front teeth and relax your jaw. With intention, breathe in slowly, deeply, and silently. Breathe out, making an audible sound, like a loud huh. Repeat three or four times. Your breath becomes the vibration that is changing your energy. I also like to breathe deeply in through my nose for a count of five, hold for a count of five, release through my pursed lips for a count of five.

    The four-seven-eight, or relaxing breath, is a "natural tranquilizer for the nervous system."[47] With your tongue pressed against the top of your back teeth where they meet the roof of your mouth, breathe in silently for a count of four, hold for a count of seven, push the breath out of your mouth with a whooshing sound for eight. Find what feels comfortable for you. Again, you are your own best judge of what feels right and what you will do on a regular basis.

4. *Create a little mantra for yourself.* Double bonus points if you also make it a positive affirmation. Make it a simple sentence that you can chant when you get stressed, and that will lift you up and calm you down. Start with: I am (and fill in the blank with something positive). Simply choose what is best for you in a given situation.

> "I accept and trust myself exactly as I am."
> "I am healthy, I am strong, I am empowered,"
> "I can do hard things."
> "I am enough, exactly as I am."
> "I deserve happiness and peace of mind."
> "I release the need to control the situation."
> "I am in control of my choices."

5. *Write a gratitude list.* Practicing gratitude is considered one of the top ways to bring added happiness to your life, and it helps keep you focused on the big picture. You recognize the tangible and intangible things that you have been given.[48] This simple act is a way to create a ritual and remind yourself it is about the journey, about the process, not about the outcome. It takes some discipline, but that's part of the journey.

6. *Spend time in nature.* As little as two hours a week of time spent in nature can have a profound effect on cognitive function and overall well-being.[49] It is not simply a luxury; it is a necessity if we are to thrive. It brings with it the desire to be physically active, which has its own health benefits.

7. *Bringing nature indoors* into your living space extends the

"feel good" benefits of being close to Mother Nature.[50] It just makes sense that the physiological and psychological benefits of spending time in nature do not stop at the front door. Frank Lloyd Wright understood that. Frank Lloyd Wright said, "*Study nature, love nature, stay close to nature. It will never fail you.*"[51] It permeated everything he designed. I talk more about this in a later chapter. The advantages of being in nature or surrounded by it, even artificially, are well documented. Visual, as well as audible exposure in art or music, does a body good.[52]

TAKEAWAYS

- Self-awareness is the greatest change agent. It is found in stillness.

- We all possess a lizard brain, also called our limiting beliefs. It is our ego feeding us "untruths" out of fear and self-doubt.

- It is important to find stress-reducing coping mechanisms.

- Connect to your body. Learn to listen to and trust how you're feeling.

- You have everything you need within.

6

SEEING WITH NEW EYES

No problem can be solved from the same level
of consciousness that created it.
—Albert Einstein

ONE PART OF THE *EGO-SELF* LIES, MANIPULATES, and tortures. Remember Jokey (the name of my limiting beliefs)? Jokey rears her ugly head when my thoughts and feelings stem from fear or insecurity. We believe the thoughts that arise, thoughts we identify with, good or bad. We learned them through past experiences, or we were taught them, but we don't have to be a victim to them when they do not serve us. They can be little energy vampires. Your "illusion of self" ego dies with self-awareness.

Our ego not only blinds us but makes us blind to what others see. Whatever we see and believe, we think others should see and believe too. Our ego is one aspect of ourselves that we identify with. It's not all bad; it doesn't have to be the enemy. Maintaining a healthy ego, like all things, is a balancing act. You must accept all sides of yourself to possess and express authenticity.[53]

You don't see things as they are; you see things as *you* are, the seeds you have sown.

You are not your weight, you are not your job, you are not your home, you are not your bank account. If you stripped everything away, all the labels, all the accomplishments, all the mistakes, who would you be? This knowledge comes from deep within: being still, spending time alone, learning to listen to your intuition. I know that for many, spending time alone feels really scary, but it is so crucial to understanding ourselves. If we show up for ourselves, then we can show up for others. Trust that the right people will show up for us, and those who are not right for us may fall away. Surrender to that.

Your authentic self is part of your ego that does not identify with "the illusion of self." It is the space between your thoughts. It is your inner truth. It is who you are at your core—you in your purest form. The only way you can tell the difference between your learned ego and your authentic self is to become skillful in using and trusting your feeling ability. You must know what your body is physically feeling and what your heart is emotionally feeling in order to expose your ego's "shoulds" and "should nots."[54] When you are willing to reveal your authentic self to others, you are allowing people to see the real you. Living from a place of authenticity leads you to bliss.

When I used to mention that I felt "stuck" in an area of my life, some snickered. I soon realized that those who snickered were somewhat more enlightened because they realized it was only a thought in my mind. My mind prison.

The Buddha said, *"Enlightenment tastes like freedom."*[55]

Whenever you have a thought that causes suffering, you are not free in your mind. The only thing that can be done is to change the thought that is creating the suffering. If I changed the thought, I could change my reality. EUREKA! I was making it true for me, and I was suffering because of it when I was thinking the thought, "I am stuck."

Your thoughts create your reality.

You can alter your reality by altering your thoughts. Sounds simple right?

Unfortunately, the thought, "I am not enough," is quite common. I would have sworn up and down and back and forth that I was not a part of that misleading club, but when I dug down deep, I realized I was. I was reinforcing the belief every time I had thoughts like "I must not be good enough because I did not get into my college of choice," or "I must not be good enough because I am not asked to sit on such or such a panel," or "I did not get the design job I was hoping for," or "I must not be good enough because I gained weight and my skinny jeans no longer fit." Blah, blah, blah. Then it hit me: I have my free will. I could choose to think different thoughts. Hallelujah!

"I love and accept myself for who I am—now and always." As I got older, I realized we don't give free will enough credit.

Every day is a new opportunity to make different choices or create a different reality for ourselves. We always have a choice.

I realized I accomplished everything I set my mind to as an adult. I have done big things, overcome hard obstacles. I am a hero on a hero's journey, and you are too. I might once have been the chubby, pimply, frizzy-haired girl who was a mediocre student (and was hard on herself), but that didn't define me, and that certainly does not describe the woman I became. I began to incorporate positive affirmations into my day to keep the positivity flowing.

> I am blazing my own trail.
> I have everything I need.
> All that I desire comes to me.
> I do big things.
> I am a strong, independent woman.
> I raised successful children.

Now you try it:

> I AM ENOUGH
> I am a loyal _____(friend, sister, brother, employee, fill
> in the blank).
> I am valuable to _____.
> I am proud of myself for_____.
> I am _____.

How does it feel in your body when you say things to yourself like, "I blaze my own trail" vs. "I am wracked with self-doubt and uncertainty?" The answer is pretty clear. If we tell ourselves negative messages, we generate a negative vibe and vice versa. We want to avoid becoming victims in our life. Victimhood has no upside. Much of this can be attributed to a lack of self-awareness. That may lead people down the path of drama-filled, defensive, chaotic behavior—you know, like the people who play the blame game believing they are always right because it is way more self-satisfying to the ego. Self-awareness is the nemesis of the ego. Ego is distraction; awareness is stillness.

Negativity Begets Negativity/Positivity Begets Positivity

I cannot tell you how many times I have witnessed the correlation between my clients' limiting beliefs and the state of chaos in their homes. I know that when we are stressed, we believe we can't always maintain the housekeeping or discipline the kids, but everything is a byproduct of everything else. In short, when you feel a great deal of negativity about yourself, it stops you from keeping up with regular tasks because your mind is too busy being occupied with the feeling that you cannot do any of these things. Feeling incapable makes you incapable at times.

Everything within your home should support the calm, peaceful feeling that is good for you, as well as anyone you live with, in terms of overall well-being. If you don't have your thoughts and beliefs sorted out, you are unwittingly passing that on to another generation if they are living with you. Kids feel all the energy in the home and in you. I remember going into my friends' homes as a kid, and although I might not have had a language for it at the time, my friends' homes that were tumultuous or seemed to house harried parents always felt uncomfortable. The energy was chaotic. I avoided spending time there.

One particular girlfriend's parents always seemed to be arguing. They would have these formal sit-down dinners. At first, I loved to get invited to dinner. It felt special, almost regal, to sit in the dining room and be served, but I eventually began to decline the invitation. Why? Because it didn't make me feel good to sit in their fancy dining room, eating off the fancy china with soft music playing in the background while nobody spoke to each other. The intention did not match the experience. The tension was palpable. There seemed to be a heaviness hanging in the air. I remember feeling it even back then, which tells me that children feel these things. My childhood girlfriend took it in stride and said, "That's just what my parents do."

In my book, that's not the lesson healthy parents pass along to their children. I lost touch with my girlfriend, but I would be curious to know what she thinks about it as an adult. How does she behave with her family, and what do their sit-down family dinners look like?

I look back on my own family's dinners with so much fondness. Granted, it was a different time, but my mother made a full meal, including dessert, and we all came running. Conversation flowed easily; my dad cracked jokes, my sister spilled something, I was probably annoyed or complaining, and my brother was his argumentative self. I miss those days. I knew they were an important part of a healthy family dynamic because I had something to compare it to.

Some of us learn what to do from our role-model parents, and some learn what not to do. We take the lessons and improve upon them or adjust them to fit our own unique lifestyles. Either way, they are valuable lessons. I made sure that when I was serving family meals that we always talked and engaged the way I had learned from my parents. We always had a family sit-down dinner. I loved to annoy my kids with the request to tell me something good and something bad about their day. It was an opportunity to bond and create further interactions.

Today, even when people still have family meals, often everyone is on their phones. This digital dialogue is no better. We are becoming an isolated society full of false relationships. Fear of missing out is misplaced. What we are missing out on is creating real, healthy connections. That's where joy and a sense of wholeness lies.

When your home is your sanctuary, you should leave stress outside the front door or have the tools to defuse it as soon as possible to maintain inner peace. Institute a digital detox, especially during mealtime. Lead by example. Words have weight, and every interaction should be mindfully executed with the understanding that your energy can be felt. Others are watching, even the tiniest of occupants.

My Home Is Not Worthy

Shelia is the "go-to person" if you are in need of anything. She is on the school board, the community leader, always the head of this and that. If you suffered a death in the family or there is an illness, Sheila is the first person at your door with a cake in hand. (Everything is better with cake, right?) Sheila is someone you call if you need a ride to the doctor or to lend an ear if you just want to vent. She makes you feel like you are the most important person in the world at that moment.

The day I stepped inside Sheila's home was the day everything changed for me where Shelia was concerned. In the distance, as I looked through the foyer and into the living room beyond, the wallpaper was curling, rather significantly, because it had peeled away from its backing, with a yellowish stain left in its place. It was literally the second thing I saw after I passed over the threshold. The flooring was chipped and worn clear down to the subfloor between the toilet and the vanity in the powder room when I excused myself to use it. I realized I had stopped breathing for a moment because the illusion of who I thought Shelia to be was shattered, as I now had a deeper understanding of her. I uncovered the message in the mess.

I was overcome with sadness. How could this lovely woman who made herself available for so many others not be available to herself? What did she not value within herself, or what negative messages had she been told and accepted about living in less-than-ideal circumstances? Where was she peeling? Where was she chipped? I felt sad for Shelia. I felt like I understood her a little better in the moment.

I had a small window into her soul. I wanted to help her. She's there for everyone else; who shows up for her? I wanted to point out what I was sensing, but it was not my place. She did not ask, and I did not offer.

I say to you: Is your home in less-than-optimal living condition? Are there repairs that need to be made, things that need to be fixed or replaced?

Take a good look around with those "eyes of a stranger" and notice everything because you can be sure others will be doing so. People will form a "mental picture" or make a judgment about who they think you are. There are many factors being considered when we sum someone up in the three to seven seconds we allow for this to take place. When someone meets you for the first time, they are observing how you carry yourself, your body language, how you are dressed, whether you exude confidence.

Your home is not unlike your physical presence. Your home is an extension of you, non-verbally saying something about you: your identity, your values, your aesthetic. We view people more positively when we experience a positive impression than if we experience a negative one. We assume that our impression of who we believe that person to be applies to all areas of their life. This is called the halo effect, which is an idea attributed to Edward Thorndike.

"The halo effect is a well-documented social psychology phenomenon that theorizes that people tend to be biased in their judgment of a person based on several personality traits. It was taken a step further to include transferring the feelings about one attribute of something to another attribute."[56] We are colored by what we see or experience first, similar to a first impression.

If the house is clean and orderly, we believe the person to be trustworthy, professional, or any attribute that is positive. If we are met with an unkempt messy home, we might assume the person is lazy or unreliable or attribute a negative impression to them. Could you be living as Sheila is living? My thought was that she didn't value herself as much as she valued others, and I wondered why.

You may never have considered the first impression your home (or office) makes, but you should. Someone is always looking.

The same goes for businesses, too. Here's another example of the halo effect that I experienced.

I saw an integrative medical doctor for a time between my Lyme disease and autoimmune diagnoses. I walked up to the front door and twice was met with pots of dead flowers. In the spring, the pansies had long since faded. I thought this was likely to be okay; it might have happened rather quickly because the temperature climbed seemingly overnight from spring to summer.

So, I let it go, but the following fall, when I again approached the front door and pots of expired mums greeted me. I was outraged!

"This is a place of healing," I heard myself shout out as I passed through the front doors. This is not a small thing! If they couldn't care for their plants, how were the doctors there going to care for me? I had to leave the practice.

Seeing with New Eyes Exercise

This is my most favorite exercise, and I think it's valuable for anyone to do and then continue to do every so often, as "good housekeeping," so you are always in control of the impression you may be conveying.

- Walk into your home through the front door as if you were a stranger or a guest in your own home. Was the curb appeal attractive?

- Was the path clear to get inside?

— Was the door attractive and easy to open?

— Are the windows clean? Can you look through them without trouble?

— How do you feel the minute you walk in the door?

— Remember the mind/body compass exercise (pg 96-97) when you go inward and ask yourself, "How does this make me feel?" Use it. Scan your body and question where your feelings fall on that scale, based on the environment you find yourself in.

— Are you struck by anything immediately: good or bad?

— Look around and notice everything. Take your time. Notice what everything looks like, how everything feels, smells, and sounds.

— Go from room to room, maybe making notes along the way. No detail is too small to be overlooked. How does standing in each part of each room feel in your body?

— Is there a heaviness or a lightness to the space? Is there adequate lighting, or does it seem dark? Do you see dust or dead flowers?

— How is the quality of the fabrics holding up? Are the fabrics faded or sun-damaged?

— What is the quality of the air you're breathing, the water you may be drinking? Are the cabinets in the kitchen clean? Is the room free of odors?

— Is the bed made?

— What about the bathroom, leaky faucets, perhaps? Leave no stone unturned, no question unanswered.

- Are there broken or chipped tchotchkes, miscellaneous items lying around that are neither here nor there?

- Could you corral collectibles or photographs into a meaningful display as opposed to having a few scattered about in different locations?

- Is all the stuff you hate holding a place among other stuff you hate: the broken things, the unloved things, the obligatory gift someone gave you long ago. Could you let it go?

- Move energy around you as you go. Clap your hands, move furniture an inch or two, rearrange objects. Small changes can lead to big results. Be open to change. Get excited.

- What is working and what is not working? Laser-focused, ask yourself, is this room the best it can be?

- Are there any areas that need attention, such as cleaning, repair, editing, a coat of paint, a little TLC? If so, make a list and get moving: Replace, Repair, or Remove.

Remember the Three R's! People are gobsmacked when they realize they had stopped seeing what was right in front of them for years. You need to set about defining what will make your heart sing, what brings visual and sensory gratification to your sacred space.

The importance of keeping things clean and ridding yourself of things that appear broken or superfluous is allowing more chi, or good energy, to flow throughout. This is always the first step when you put a mindful practice into pride of place. Keeping the energy up increases the life force, and everything grows exponentially: prosperity, abundance, and harmony.

TAKEAWAYS

- Your authenticity comes from a deep knowledge and acceptance of yourself, without all the labels and attachments.

- Your value comes from being, not doing.

- With acceptance comes the ability to be comfortable in your own skin.

- Positive affirmations and gratitude beget positivity.

- Turn thoughts of negativity and those that cause suffering around for a more positive perspective.

- Your home holds this stress and negativity in the form of blocked energy. When you eliminate it energetically and become more abundant of mind, your home, in turn, becomes a vessel for an abundance of spirit.

7

LOVE THE ONE YOU'RE WITH

What lies behind us and what lies before us are tiny matters
compared to what lies within us.
—Henry S. Haskins

To feel self-worth is to feel self-love, to be validated by no one else but you. Self-worth is at the core of our very selves—our thoughts, feelings, and behaviors are intimately tied into how we view our worthiness and value as human beings. You are worthy by the mere fact that you are here. Step into your power. Strut your stuff. Boldly go where you may not have gone before. Kick the limiting beliefs and negative self-talk to the curb.

We all have gifts that we bring into the world. We all do some things well and other things, maybe not so much. Play to your strengths. Be a rock star in that area of your life. Feeling good about yourself has muscle memory. When something (or someone) comes along and tries to knock you down, your self-worth is what picks you back up, allows you to shake it off, and gets you back out there.

Maybe you need to show yourself forgiveness. Maybe you need a dose of compassion toward others and especially toward yourself. Awareness is once again the key to exploring what needs to happen in order for you to move freely and authentically through life. If you hold on and repress what causes pain within, you could end up sick, literally sick. Your physical cells sense what is going on in your body; your body senses what is going on in your mind.

Another technique to achieve this awareness is by writing yourself a letter. First, write it speaking as the child within you. What does that child need to hear in order to heal or grow or feel unconditionally loved? When we identify what we need, we can learn to give it to ourselves. We are soul healing.

Next, speak to the present you from your future self. What wisdom does your future self have to impart to you? Think of him or her as your inner shaman, the older, wiser, future you that only has your best interest in mind. This healer, mentor, teacher, guider of love and light wants nothing more than to connect you with your best self. When you find yourself questioning or struggling, ask yourself, "What would my inner shaman say or do? What direction would he/ she point me in?" More often than not, things are less complicated than we make them out to be. From that vantage point, we may adopt a "this too shall pass" mentality that helps ease the feeling of being overwhelmed. Where are your joys, where are your struggles? How can you move closer to or away from them? How could you integrate them?

The love you are seeking is already within you. When you realize your own self-worth, healing and growth appear. You rise.

Just as with your own physical body, if you want your home to convey your authentic self, you need to understand who you believe yourself to be at your core, away from the labels. However, there is nothing wrong with becoming attached to labels if they serve your highest purpose and you want to convey to others what you value. People who value themselves also value the things around them, such as where they dwell and who they associate with. There is a saying that we become most like the five people we spend the most time with. Who are you surrounded by most of the time? What are their values?

Using myself as an example, among my own core values is a love of beauty: I love beautiful art. Granted, my definition of beauty may differ from yours, but what I see as beautiful enters my home along with everything else that matches who I believe I am expressing myself to be. Other core values that I embody are uniqueness, communication, and a sense of sharedness. I value those qualities in others as well. With that in mind, I like materials in my home that have an innate authenticity because they reflect back those qualities that I value. I like gold as a color and as a material. I am a Leo, after all. That shade signifies a luxe material and heightened drama. I do love a little drama, the good kind.

High self-worth individuals take time and put effort into nurturing the things around them because they understand those things contribute to a better sense of overall well-being. They value that because they value their health and happiness.

I have a friend whose greatest quality is a childlike wonder. She loves fantasy and has a very curious nature and thirst for knowledge. She loves her friends and family fiercely. Would it surprise you that I would describe her home as a living museum of curiosities, books, and photos spilling from all corners of her home, representing her journey? Her home is a collage of her life: mementos, collections that have been building for years from places near and far. Details abound like living art throughout the house, spanning a life's story told in bits and pieces of pottery, art, color, and fiber.

I have another friend who has multiple homes made up with antiques, secondhand finds, inherited pieces, all with a touch of whimsy, including colorful wooden furniture juxtaposed with and giving weight to delicate wrought iron furniture. Where I see spindly and mismatched, she sees a maker's hand, integrity, and love. Everything tells you the story of who she is: a collector, a nurturer, a creator, and a people pleaser. She has strong ties to her heritage and has created vignettes from all sorts of trinkets that friends bestowed on her as gifts over the years. Whimsy and fantasy coexist in an environment of my friend's making. It communicates her loving heart and the bonds she has built.

If you had to write a story, even just a few sentences, describing your home and how you have expressed yourself within it, what would you say, and what would the reader learn about you? Would it tell a reader who you are? Would they understand what you value?

Connecting your home to your authentic self happens when your beliefs, thoughts, desires, values, motives, strengths, and environment are aligned. Authenticity is the ability to accept yourself for all challenges and triumphs, shadows and light, and to be willing to show others. You have to be willing to be vulnerable. We show our vulnerability and what makes us joyful. We show our flaws almost as easily as we show our strengths because we understand and accept them as part of the equation. We surround ourselves with people who accept us, all the parts of us. We show ourselves, for that is how we can really be accepted for ourselves. That is such a gift.

If we crave authenticity from others, why wouldn't we offer it in return? These are happy, well-adjusted people who have educated themselves on the topics of worthiness and introspection. Maybe you are not there yet. Maybe you need more tools in your toolbox to inform you how your mind mimics your living space. What if you have not figured out your purpose or passion? What if your home is spectacularly clean, but your mind does not follow suit?

If I told you there was a way out of suffering, would you want to know what it was so you could put it into practice right away? I hope your answer is "yes."

Start by turning your thoughts around. I say this a lot: change your perspective, and your life changes. I often use this tool when I am coaching a client. It can have such a profound effect on helping you "ease" out of the idea that your thoughts are *the* thoughts that make a situation true (for you).

Your belief about the thought can cause suffering. For so long, I wondered why someone else did not see a specific situation the same way I saw it. Was it possible that the other person had a different perspective? I couldn't fathom it. The more I questioned why, why, why, the more I suffered. My expectation did not show up in reality. That always causes frustration and disappointment.

Allowing our minds to argue with reality, asking those "what ifs," or "why nots," wanting reality to be different than it is, is pointless. We benefit from reframing our thoughts. Reframing allows us to look at a thought from a different perspective. Shifting from a thought that may cause internal suffering to a reframed thought that allows us to see the thought from a more positive perspective is the equivalent of making lemonade from lemons. We become kinder to ourselves and feel freer when we can observe our thoughts, not attach to them, and allow for the possibility that we can change the meaning. This is another way in which we remove mental clutter, so we can see the truth in a fundamental way. Do we as humans like to suffer? No, of course not.

If you have a thought that makes you unhappy, dissatisfied, hurt, angry, or confused, write it down (in its simplest terms), for example:

Thought: My spouse does not enjoy spending time with me.

That thought could cause you to suffer. Perhaps you feel like you and your spouse do not share the same interests or hobbies. He or she complains when doing something they are not enjoying instead of making a concerted effort to rally behind your enthusiasm. Worse yet, you spend much time apart or engaging in separate activities. You complain and maybe fight about it, feeling isolated from each other. That leads to loneliness. You each spend time alone in separate parts of the house, creating an even bigger void.

Can you turn that thought around? Instead of saying and believing these words:

"My spouse does not enjoy spending time with me."

Turn the thought around to: "My spouse does enjoy spending time with me."

Now give me a few examples to support the statement, "My spouse does enjoy spending time with me." Here are a few:

1. Last week we went to a park. After a long, pleasant sunset walk, we sat by a lake and toasted marshmallows in a fire pit. "We haven't had s'mores in years," you happily reminisced. "That was enjoyable."

2. Aha! So there are things you like to do together. What else? Can you name a few more things you and your spouse like to do together?

3. We like to go sailing.

4. We love to spend time reading to our children.

5. We enjoy debating each other over current events.

These are all good examples of things you enjoy together. Maybe you can concentrate on doing something you both enjoy at least once a week (or whatever is the best time frame for you), and you find ways to enjoy your alone time away from each other without going into a state of all-or-nothing thinking.

Maybe after careful examination and introspection—and a good life coach—you realize what you have been feeling is the thought: "I don't enjoy spending time with me." But instead, you were expressing or projecting the thought as: "My spouse doesn't enjoy spending time with me."

The second statement makes you a victim with no control. The other, truer, statement is more empowering and allows you to make the necessary shifts for greater self-satisfaction.

Let's unpack that a little further. Give me a few examples of how you don't enjoy spending time with yourself. Perhaps you might say something like:

1. I don't go to the movies or dinner alone. It's not as much fun as being with others.

2. I'm a people person. I always enjoy being with others more than my own company.

3. I feel anxious and stressed when I'm alone.

4. I have friends that do solo traveling. I would never do that! How much fun could that really be?

I want you to consider these questions: Why wouldn't you be comfortable being alone? What is the worst that could happen? Do you really care what people think? What are you afraid of?

You might come up with different answers or realize you never thought of your reaction in those ways. You might find yourself saying things like: I am not good at being alone; it makes me uncomfortable. I'd feel like a loser, and people would make assumptions about why I was alone. I feel like I might need a companion to validate me. I feel lonely when I am alone. I busy myself so I do not have to think too much. I don't like being in my head.

These are all things someone might say after evaluating the thought: "I don't enjoy spending time with me."

It's different for everyone, of course.

What do you think is at the root of this feeling?

Did something happen that caused you to feel this way?

Did someone leave you alone or make you feel bad about being alone?

Do you have enough self-confidence to trust your instincts?

Did you ever experience doing something alone?

You'd be surprised how many people assume they wouldn't like something before they've even tried it. Having the ability to spend time alone is a foundation for cultivating a relationship with your authentic self and standing in your own power.

Reframing or turning thoughts around allows you to begin to start a dialogue on any issue that creates dissatisfaction to get to the root cause of the feeling. Pay attention to how your body feels when you think a thought that creates suffering. Could this feeling somehow express itself in the environment of your home as well? Use your mind/body compass to scan where you fall physically and mentally on the mind/body compass meter. This will lead to awareness, which will lead to the opportunity for you to make a change.

Next, turn your thought around again, from the original "my spouse doesn't enjoy spending time with me" to "I do not enjoy spending time with my spouse."

A few examples would be:

1. I do not like shopping with him/her. My spouse makes me feel guilty about spending money.
2. I do not like traveling with him/her. Everything is a problem, and my spouse complains a lot.

3. I do not like playing sports with him/her. My significant other is too competitive, and it takes the joy out of the experience.

Could your spouse feel as though you don't enjoy his or her company? Did you balk at these kinds of events in the past or go with your friends instead? Can you see where your spouse might have thought you would have a better time if you were without him or her?

This exercise is playful. You are trying on statements that may be true or truer than the thoughts in your head. You are validating another way of thinking about a situation. It can get a little philosophical. That's when it really gets fun.

After all, you are reframing the thoughts that create suffering as thoughts that give you freedom from suffering. We are not meant to suffer but, oh, how some of us create so much of it. We can be our own worst enemy. Retraining your brain to tell yourself a different story, without the suffering, is soothing to the soul.

This work, doing the turnarounds that I am describing here, is based on a program called The Work, by Byron Katie.[57] The author's process is more extensive than what I have laid out here. The program is a rich, detailed, nuanced process. Katie has countless free resources and demonstrations on her site. I highly recommend it to you.

Reframing is one of the most profound ways I have discovered to take the power out of your thoughts. Katie's work is truly groundbreaking. She teaches that suffering is optional, and she teaches it freely to anyone who cares to learn it and improve the condition of their life.

Can you see how if you change the thoughts in your head and your attachment to the thoughts that cause you suffering, your life could get better? If your life gets better, you behave differently. People around you respond differently, not because they have changed but because you have. When you want a situation to change, you must start from within.

You will see that if everything around you, including relationships, gets better, then it will seem logical that you want to spend more time doing things and being with those who enrich you and spend more time in spaces that enrich you. You would consciously create more enriching spaces to occupy, and everything would feel like it is in alignment.

You are more aware of how you show up in the world because you have set your reality up to be in alignment with your positive attitude, surrounded by others who reflect it back. The universe also loves gratitude. The more grateful you feel, the more you will have to feel grateful about. It's like the question of the chicken or the egg again. We don't know which came first, but does it matter? Dive in.

Once you have this knowledge, you have the power. When you know better, you can do better. Once you are in alignment, you will do what it takes to always be in alignment—in mind, body, spirit, and in your living space. That will keep you going in the direction of your North Star.

Having this knowledge and power is crucial for your self-worth. That self-worth is the foundation for self-empowerment and overall well-being. It impacts our decisions, how we treat ourselves, and how we invite others to treat us. Be mindful of filling your brain *not* with negative self-talk but with uplifting, positive life-affirming thoughts instead.

Remember what I've said before—I can't stress this enough: we truly believe that we are what we think and speak, so if we focus on the countless hardships that life is throwing our way, all we will get is more hardships. On the flip side, if we begin our days with a grateful heart, focusing on the blessings in our lives and the positive things we wish to bring into our world, the universe will reflect back to us the positive energy that we are emitting.

Because I had high self-worth, back when I was lying in bed feeling dissatisfied, I knew I deserved more than I was receiving. I didn't need to settle for that tiny TV deep in an armoire. I was not aligned with my desire.

Having the level of self-worth that allowed me to think this means thinking highly of yourself and having an unwavering belief that you are good just the way you are, regardless of the opinions of others, regardless of difficult situations you may find or have found yourself in. You are not defined by others but rather by what you know to be true about yourself deep within.

I must add a huge caveat here—everyone makes mistakes. We have limitations, flaws, shadows; we are human, after all. We know these things about ourselves, and we accept them. Each of us is on a different path. Not good or bad, just different.

Regardless, I knew that changing my experience—because it would make me happier— was all the information I needed to move toward that which actually made me happier. My self-worth equaled what I felt I deserved.

Similarly, you may sometimes feel that you're not worthy; therefore you accept things that you don't have to. I have heard clients say, I don't deserve something or that it's too extravagant. That tells me that, deep within, they might have some work to do around self-worth. This extends to any area of your life, not just the features in your home.

However, if you train your brain to tell yourself a more empowering thought, thereby raising your vibrational energy to, "I am worthy, I am worth it, I deserve this, I am good enough," then you will never settle for "less than" in any area of your life because you are vibrating higher.

A vibration is a state of being. Even if you do not understand the concept or have not mastered the awareness around it yet, you do feel it. It is the basis of the law of attraction: "Where your thoughts go, energy flows."

If thoughts feel heavy or dark, they do not serve you, and you will generate more heavy, dark thoughts. If you become mindful of thinking thoughts that empower you, uplift you, make you feel brighter and lighter, you will begin to manifest that kind of thinking. Each time you catch yourself thinking a thought that creates suffering or negativity, identify it and turn it around.

If going from "I am not worthy" to "I am worthy" feels like too big a leap, take a smaller step. Tell yourself:

- I am working on mastering this concept.

- This is a process, and I am moving forward.

- I am capable and am working toward my goal

- My path is moving me forward.

Tell yourself any empowering thought that will keep you in a state of positivity and possibility. You're essentially developing a new habit, which requires a consistent change in behavior over time. The process may not be easy, but the reward is worth it. Manifesting an outward expression of your healthier thoughts and behaviors leads to a better sense of "self," well-being, and fulfillment.

As you master this new positive skill, your mind has muscle memory. Living from a place of self-worth translates to other areas of your life.

I've found that my self-worth dictates that I want the best for myself.

I'm worthy, therefore:

- I will accept only healthy foods that fuel me and are good for my healthy body.

- I will live in an environment that is clean, in good repair, and brings me joy.

- I will be mindful of that which keeps me on my path to wholeness, fulfillment, and happiness.

- I will release anything that is in opposition to this manifesto.

Working as I do, both with interior design and as a life coach, I know for a fact that when you care about your home, you will care about yourself. Therefore, it is more likely that you will also care for yourself.

I've found that we tend to believe our negative mind more than our positive one. I don't know why it is easier to believe the negative thoughts than the positive ones, but it is time to change that way of thinking.

Stop, Drop, and Roll

In this exercise, for every negative thought you have about yourself:

- STOP and recognize it.

- DROP in two or more positive thoughts to replace the negative one.

- ROLL with the new, more upbeat thoughts. Let your mind absorb that which enhances your well-being and does not diminish it.

- Reflect on how much better that feels within your mind and body.

Make a list of all the things that make you awesome: characteristics, qualities, virtues, things you are good at, things that come easy, what others might say they like about you. For example: I am a good communicator. I am a loyal friend. I am compassionate and sensitive. I have nice eyes. My curiosity takes me to interesting places. I work hard on myself to improve my reality on a daily basis. I have great style. I find humor in difficulty. I make a mean banana bread. And so on and so on and so on….keep going. You have thousands of terrific characteristics! Dazzle yourself! Then remind yourself daily about your fabulousness.

Because, as the saying goes, *"The words you speak become the house you live in,"* you always want to be impeccable with your words. Words are building blocks. We are mindfully building up, not knocking down.

Having high self-worth is one of the most important principles you need for building a strong foundation and vibrating on a higher frequency. With a good blueprint, shop drawings, and sheathing, you can shore up the framework of your inner space.

Remember, to raise your self-worth, you should raise your personal vibration, using the "I am" prefix with positive affirmations and mantras.

I am…worthy.

I am…resilient,

I am…good enough.

I am…a great problem solver.

Ask yourself, "How would I behave if I put myself first?"

What would I accept and not accept if I were No. 1?

What choices would I make that would align with myself as No. 1?

What would my inner shaman say? What advice would be given?

Here's another exercise for you:

When you hold yourself in high regard and know your worth, you only accept things into your life that support this. And whenever you have a negative thought, you're usually your own worst critic. The solution is to turn those thoughts around.

Instead of "I don't deserve this," say, "I do deserve this, and here's why…."

Instead of "I am overweight," say, "I love my body unconditionally and here's why…."

Instead of saying "I am unlovable," say, "I am so lovable, and here's why…."

Instead of "I am not good enough as I am," say, "I am good enough just the way I am, and here's why…."

Then give yourself three examples (or more) of why you are worthy, lovable…whatever.

Guess what, just by the mere fact that you are here, on this planet, reading this book, "you are worth it!"

Ask yourself thought-provoking questions:

1. What is something that no one could ever take away from me?

2. Who am I, and who am I not?

3. What kind of person do others expect me to be?

4. What does self-worth mean to me?

5. What false ideas have I been taught about myself?

6. What external things don't define my self-worth?

7. If I lost everything in my life, what would I still have that would be of value?[58]

Successful people have a morning routine that helps them start their day on the right foot. I want to be that person. Every morning I swing my legs off the side of the bed, say a little prayer, and feel gratitude. I breathe deeply; then I repeat a few phrases that I am working on that I want to instill in myself. "I am blessed to be doing what I love, I am in good health, I am a best-selling author." Every few months, I change the mantra. It's a gratitude-intention setting-positive affirmation-manifestation list rolled up into one. Now you try it. Go claim your power.

TAKEAWAYS

- Feeling worthy is a byproduct of deep discovery and acceptance.

- When questioning something, ask yourself, "What would my inner shaman say or do?"

- The growth is in the challenge. Challenge yourself!

- Practice positive affirmations whenever negativity slips in. Stop, Drop, and Roll.

- Change your perspective to shift out of suffering.

- Create a ritual for yourself that aligns with your desires.

- Having high self-worth allows you to love yourself unconditionally because you understand you are fundamentally worthy.

- High self-worth manifests in living authentically, aligned with your values.

8

ENERGETICALLY SPEAKING

If you want to know the secrets of the Universe, think in terms of energy, frequency and vibration.

—Nikola Tesla

HAVE YOU EVER MET SOMEONE AND THOUGHT, "I like their vibe?" Some people give off an energy of positivity and joy, and you feel a sense of connectedness toward them right away. Some people just exude "light." It's a bit like catching magic in a bottle. You are vibrating at a higher frequency and calling in the same. "Your vibe attracts your tribe," has become a well-known quote attributed to motivational speaker Jim Rohn. He also coined the phrase, "You are the average of the five people you spend the most time with."

When you surround yourself with people who share similar goals and values, you lift each other up. You are motivated to be a better person because you admire and are inspired by those close to you. Careful, if you spend time with people who are negative or who play the victim, it can bring you down too. Surround yourself with like-minded people or those you aspire to be more like. That creates more fulfilling relationships and a positive attitude because we know fulfilling relationships are good for our well-being.

Have you ever been in an environment where you felt completely calm and good, but maybe you didn't easily understand why? Conversely, have you ever had a less than desirable reaction to a person or place and were miffed about it but didn't know the cause? Have you ever recoiled immediately because something sucked all the energy out of you or the room? That's vibrational energy.

Everything is made up of electromagnetic energy vibrating at different frequencies that correspond to sound, light, and color. Chi, the energetic vital life force of all living things, is balanced or unbalanced; what the Chinese call *qi* is anglicized as chi.[59] The term *prana* may be used in Hinduism—it means the same thing—the source of everything, the energy of life, the building block of all things.[60] To understand chi and to live in harmony and balance with the chi within your body and your environment is to live an emotionally, physically, spiritually, spatially balanced life.

Chi exists between and within us and the universe. Creating a healthy, supportive environment that nourishes our body, mind, and spirit means we must also be mindful of the chi that exists all around us, including within the walls of our home. When the flow is in a positive state, it slowly meanders and drifts effortlessly like a brook. When the flow is in a negative state, energy is stagnant or blocked, like a dam holding back the flow; in this case, it is the flow of energy. Eastern wisdom has been influenced by chi for more than 4,000 years.[61] It is recognized as the balance of yin and yang (female and male, positive and negative electromagnetic energy), which flows through everything in creation.[62] You need both for balance. One without the other creates an imbalance.

To quote from the Traditional Chinese Medicine World Foundation:

> "Yin energy is feminine, earth, still, cool, dark (night), soft, intuitive, reflective, passive, accepting, and provides the quiet strength of spirit.
>
> Yang is masculine, heaven, active, hot, bright (day), hard, active, dynamic. It provides the strength of physical power.
>
> Together they are complementary and balanced. Each needs the other for wholeness. Yin and yang's dynamic flow is always in motion, always recalibrating to keep energy in harmony. They bring life to our minds, spirits, and bodies. When they are out of balance, they become negative forces that rob us of life and spirit. Keeping them in balance in our lives means keeping them in balance in our environments so that together they form healthy energy that can move freely and not become either too yin or too yang, and thus destructive."[63]

The atoms in our bodies—and the rest of the universe as well— are in a constant state of connecting or repelling, in other words, creating energy waves. Those energy waves can be measured and their effects can be seen. To better understand this, we need a short science lesson. Western ideology is somewhere between the ideas of Socrates saying that energy, or soul, is separate from matter and that the universe is made of energy to Newtonian physics, which says that the whole universe is matter and nothing else, to the more recent ideas of quantum physics which states, the atom is composed of nothing but an invisible force field which emits electrical energy, that there is nothing but energy waves. It says, "the atom is a minuscule invisible force field, a kind of a mini-tornado, which emits waves of electrical energy."[64] [65]

Those energy waves can be measured, and their effects can be seen, but they are not a material reality; they have no substance because they are, well, just energy. So, science now embraces the idea that the universe is made of energy. We are made up of atoms, and atoms continuously give off and absorb light and energy. Every cell in our body contains atoms with a negative and positive charge, each rendering the other electrically neutral. We are like living, breathing batteries! This energy, too, is considered chi, the life-force energy of the universe. Its presence is felt in every living thing. It is within us and, for a certain distance, outside of us, and a certain radius around us.

The energy in and around us affects us deeply on so many levels, whether we are aware of it or not. We want to ensure that everything in and around us aligns with our highest vision for ourselves. We need to consciously examine what is residing within us. Then we can decide what we want to keep and cultivate and what we want to release.

Understanding some of these principles gives us the knowledge to move forward toward transformation. To be conscious of the energy within our living space, we must ensure that the energy allows us to subtly shift the energetic vibrations within our environment to create a space where we thrive.

The way your home is arranged absolutely affects your life. A healthy, free-flowing space allows for ideas to flow: you can grow, you can flourish, you can create. That means that the book you are reading now, the chair you sit on, the house you live in, the Earth you live on—that so-called solid reality—consists, for the most part, of empty space. The beautiful thing is, we can fill that space with positive energy, white light, and good vibrations.

This House Just Doesn't Say Us!

Kay was a newlywed who was ready to tackle the project of making her new house a home for herself and her husband, Kenny. This adorable 30-something couple was eager to tell me about how they met and what they hoped the future would bring. They hadn't given their design aesthetic much thought. They had been focused on each other and their respective careers, so the look of their home and how they wanted it to function was not very high on their list of priorities—until now. All they could tell me was that something was "off." They couldn't say more than that about it, and when pressed, replied, "It's just a feeling we have when we walk into the house. We don't know why. A weird vibe."

They couldn't explain it, but Kay was especially sensitive to the indescribable way she felt in the large open living room, dining room, kitchen. I was standing in their great room and could not help but notice there was an inordinate amount of "old-fashioned" mahogany and oak furniture. The kind you see in your grandparents' very traditional home—or in a consignment store relegated to a distant corner because it is not the look people are attracted to these days.

I asked Kay about the origin of all the furniture and if she wanted to incorporate it into the design of her starter dream interior, and, more importantly, if it meant something to her. It is not at all uncommon for young people starting out to grab all the inherited, passed along, hand-me-down, cast-off furniture they can wrangle from friends and family members to fill a home. Was there any significance to these pieces? Did they hold a certain sentimental value, or were they expensive antiques that I should be aware of?

Kay started by telling me about the dining room set that had belonged to Kenny's grandparents. There was a heavy oak, double-pedestal table with turned legs and carved feet that had ornate lines and a rustic country look. The set included four Windsor-style chairs with their characteristic "bow" backs made of spindles or dowels and seats carved in wood to fit your posterior shape. In the family room sat a heavy brown leather, rolled-arm sofa—more than a few years past its prime—in a place of pride in front of the fireplace with mismatched gold chenille chairs on either side. A waist-high chest with brass ring hardware and a square, dark brown parsons desk sat on either side of the fireplace. The desk was Kay's paternal grandfather's; her mother had given her the chest that belonged to her when she was a girl. Those pieces just confused the situation even further because they were not telling me who this couple was.

Did any of this express Kay or Kenny? The short answer was no. Did Kay and Kenny know what they liked and did not like? Again, no, they had never really given it much thought. Kenny did talk of the memories he had of sitting at the dining table at his grandparents' house with his family. It seemed to bring him joy to recall these memories, so I thought it fair to maintain the connection he felt while trying to figure out how to honor any vision Kay might eventually express for the room.

We talked about the importance of expressing identity and desires through the design of a home. This can be especially challenging for newlyweds as they go from being individuals to being a couple, each with their own beliefs, experiences, and memories that inform their likes and dislikes.

Kenny and Kay needed to do their own deep dive to find the style that best expressed who they are. What could and would they get rid of, and what were their non-negotiables? They (and you) do not have to live with things that do not express your identity just because they were free or because you might feel guilty or obligated in some way.

The Windsor chairs stayed. That was our jumping-off point. I knew that would make Kenny happy. They're classic for a reason! We painted them black. That would make Kay happy. And they looked amazing, paired with a glass table with its shiny, new, contemporary slant.

The kids clung to the look of their traditional roots, but we added modern pieces to make everything feel younger, fresher. Now the furnishings pleased them equally. A fresh coat of white paint immediately made the rooms feel brighter and lighter, as did the sleek marble coffee table.

Out went the old sofa, in came a more streamlined mid-century style with squared arms and tufting on short steel legs that immediately opened up the space visually. Now there was space between the floor and the bottom of the sofa. We streamlined the lighting by replacing the brass fixtures that came with the place and reupholstered the mismatched gold chairs in cotton velvet with a bold graphic in black, blue, and ivory.

The place went from drab to fab without breaking the bank, and Kay and Kenny were ecstatic that they were able to get in touch with their inner aesthetic. They communicated and made compromises, all the while learning more about themselves and each other. The outcome thrilled them. How do you think they will now feel in this space they created together?

Can you imagine the change in their energy each time they walked into their new space? They did not have to live in a muddled brown environment full of dark, traditional furniture that carried the questionable energy of its past lives. I gave them the permission to explore, and explore they did, learning more about themselves—individually and as a couple—along the way.

Clearing Out Old Energy

Environments hold good or bad energy, and so can the things we add into a space. Energetic resonances are not unusual, especially with inherited and antique furniture. Those pieces had a past life with past owners. It is possible that items can absorb the energy of the occupants of a home, so can a structure. These things have become imprinted with the energy of others. Energetically, everything that ever happens in a building goes out in ripples, like the effect of a stone being thrown into a pond. The energy is recorded in the walls, floor, ceiling, furniture, fabrics, and other objects in the place.

Space clearing, as the name implies, is the act of clearing a space of any unwanted or negative energy. You want to move energy around, shifting it from undesirable to desirable and keeping it that way. This is crucial when moving into a new home or after a fight or when you bring an antique into your space, but it also makes sense to maintain the practice periodically as a good housekeeping technique. Not only does it clear a space (or things) of past occupants' imprinted energy, but it helps shift any lingering energy from those occupants that might be impeding good vibes.

The goal always is to free yourself from bad vibes, unpleasant energy, illness, anything that might be considered negative, and instead bring love and lightness into your living space.

It is not uncommon to get knocked off balance, and you continually want to bring yourself back to the state of balance to create a supportive environment for yourself and your family. Because we are energetically connected to the place where we live, space clearing our home (and ourselves) is one of the most effective ways to "lift and shift" energy that might be throwing things off balance. Think of it as a spiritual spring cleaning.

As I tell my clients, space clearing is good:

- when moving into a new home or any new beginnings.

- when you bring antiques or inherited things into your home.

- when you feel stuck.

- when you feel blah or sad, and you need a recharge.

- when you are undergoing any major life change or trauma.

- if there has been an illness.

- when you've experienced a death.

- if there has been an argument.

- when you have experienced negativity (within or outside of) the home.

- when too much overstimulation has occurred within the home.

It can help:

- clear negativity.

- bring about clarity.

- open you up to new opportunities.

— aid in abundance.

— lift spirits and shifts your state of mind.

— create positive energy.

— boost a "feel good" state.

Activating Energy Exercises

1. Open the windows and let the fresh air in. It's a great way to get the airflow circulating and to move the stagnant energy around.

2. Clean an item with soap and water.

3. Dust and clean pieces with a little natural lemon cleaner. This can have a positive effect on removing negative energy.

4. Dance, move your body, shake it all about to move energy, and "clear the cobwebs."

5. Use sound, like clapping or a singing bowl, to break up stagnant space. Use a little drum or rattle. This works equally well if your body is feeling lethargic.

6. Place crystals in an area where you want to bring a more desirable vibrational energy.

7. Place objects with movement or living things into your space, like flowers, plants, or a water feature—living things require our attention, so doing this brings naturally positive energy into the area. If you cannot add anything live, such as a fish or flowers, representational pictures will do.

8. Place a bowl of Himalayan salt near doors or windows, let it rest there for about a day, or try a Himalayan salt lamp.

SMUDGING

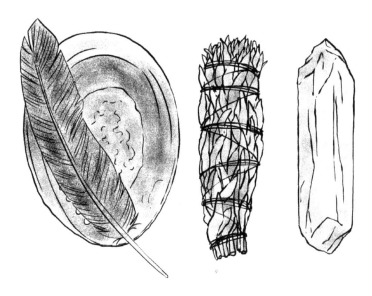

The physical act of smudging, or saging, is an ancient and sacred exercise rooted in many cultural traditions but most closely related to the Native Americans.[66] It is a symbolic practice combined with purposeful intention. It is the act of wafting a burning bundle of plants or herbs, which is called a smudge stick, that is meant to cleanse a space. As the smoke fills the room, it replaces the unwanted negative energy. It is one of the most common but powerful ways to cleanse the mind, body, spirit, and home.

Conflict, anger, illness, negativity, "stuckness," and more are absorbed in the smoke and released back out into the atmosphere. Your goal is to bring fresh, vibrant, healthy energy into the space by setting an intention and creating a ceremony around the act.

Gather your supplies:

- candle, preferably white for purity

- smudge stick

- lighter (it is said that matches interfere with the smudge smoke)

- feather (optional) to fan the smoke around the room, or you just wave the smudge stick

- abalone shell or fireproof bowl (to extinguish the stick when finished)

To begin:

- Make sure your house is free from clutter.

- Open windows, preferably on a nice day. This gives the bad energy and smoke an escape route while allowing fresh air in.

- You might want to disconnect any smoke alarms before you begin. Don't forget to reconnect the alarms when you are done.

- Light the candle and set your intention. Create a little mantra or prayer to say around the intention or desired outcome. For example, you might ask that the house and rooms be cleansed of all negative energies, thoughts, ideas, or attachments. *May balance, health, and happiness be restored.* You can adapt the mantra accordingly.

- Light the smudge stick and let it smolder for a moment. Begin by directing the smoke at your feet and moving it up your body, over and around your head, and back down your body again while taking a few deep breaths. Visualize yourself being enveloped in gentle, loving energy as a great white light consumes the space.

– Move around your home reciting your mantra. That helps keep you focused. Gently wave the smudge stick in the air, carefully allowing the smoke to drift into all areas of your home, paying particular attention to those areas that may be particularly stagnant or a location where negativity might have pooled. I like to start at the furthest point in the house, but some people start at the front door. As always, I believe you should do what feels natural for you.

– Follow the lines of door and window openings, air vents, and closets as you wave the smudge stick around with your hand or a feather. Be mindful of keeping the smudge stick over your fireproof bowl throughout the ceremony to catch cinders. We don't want any accidents.

– Visualize the negative energy being pushed out of the space, above and beyond the doors, walls, windows, and the ceiling. Picture it being replaced with a bright, positive, loving energy.

– When you have moved through your house and included spaces like the laundry room, basement, and attic, return to where you began.

– Drop the smudge stick into your fireproof bowl, applying a bit of pressure to extinguish it.

– Offer a moment of gratitude for what has taken place and the energy shift that occurred. Don't overthink any of this; there is no right or wrong way to do what comes naturally to you.

How do I know what smudging stick I should choose? It is said that "the smoke from different types of plants changes the molecular structure of air and energy inducing a cleansing effect."[67]

Here are some choices:

> Sage: General purification, cleanses all energy, calms, and heals. The best-known smudging material. It also has antimicrobial properties.
>
> Palo santo: Spanish for "holy wood."[68] Lends itself to creativity, releases negative energy, cleanses, and brings in good energy.
>
> Sweetgrass: Attracts positive energy. It is an uplifting plant with a sweet smell.
>
> Lavender: Restores balance and creates a peaceful atmosphere. It attracts loving energy, calms, and reduces stress.
>
> Cedar: Most deeply purifying, especially for clearing negative emotions (perfect for antiques, inherited items) and attracting positive energy. It attracts a grounding energy.
>
> Juniper: Used to purify and create a safe and sacred space. It is used to invigorate the mind and body.
>
> Yerba santa: Used to purify and to set and protect boundaries, especially good for self-care routines.
>
> Rosemary: A powerful healer that brings clarity to problems and helps promote new habits and fresh starts.

*If you can't or don't want to burn dried plant material, you can purchase a smudge mist or make your own. To make your own smokeless smudge mist, fill an amber glass spray bottle with purified water and add a few drops of organic sage or palo santo oil along with other essential oils. If you desire, some pink Himalayan sea salt can be added as well. I have taken to using this practice. While I love the ritual and aroma of smudge stick, new fire safety requirements have caused me to set off many a fire alarm.

A SMUDGING PRAYER

May your hands be cleansed, that they create beautiful things.

May your feet be cleansed, that they might take you where you most need to be.

May your heart be cleansed, that you might hear its messages clearly.

May your throat be cleansed, that you might speak rightly when words are needed.

May your eyes be cleansed, that you might see the signs and wonders of the world.

May this person and space be washed clean by the smoke of these fragrant plants.

And may that same smoke carry our prayers, spiraling, to the heavens.[69]

Once you have cleansed your space, you can use aromatherapy or essential oils to call in a desired energy.

Essential Oils

Snipping lilacs to place in a vase, peeling a ripe orange, ripping fresh basil to add to a recipe—aside from these being a few of my favorite things, they all release a strong, distinct scent: nature's aromatherapy. Aromatherapy is the inhalation of essential oils. Essential oils are extracts or compounds gathered from plants, flowers, seeds, roots, or fruits. These natural plant extracts have been used for thousands of years for their known healing properties. As Joanie Yanusas says, "Plants carry millions of years of wisdom in their cells, making them excellent allies in our modern lives."[70] Hippocrates, commonly referred to as the "Father of Medicine," studied the effects of essential oils on health and promoted their use for medicinal benefits. We also have Hippocrates to thank for the fundamental idea of "holism," to treat the body as one.[71]

Essential oils have been shown to have a wealth of proven health benefits. Using them is both an art and science, taking naturally extracted aromatic essences from plants to balance, harmonize, and enhance the health of body, mind, and spirit. Their use seeks to unify physiological, psychological, and spiritual processes to promote an individual's innate healing without the unwanted side effects of stronger drugs. With a change of a scent, you can change your mood or the energy in a space. These aromatic compounds also have the power to reduce anxiety and stress, quiet the mind, improve productiveness, help with minor aches and pains, or set a romantic mood.

The oil captures each plant's "essence." Aromatherapy is thought to work by stimulating smell receptors in the nose, which then send messages through the nervous system to the limbic system—the part of the brain that controls emotions. As Dr. Brent A. Bauer wrote for Mayo Clinic, "Diffusing essential oils releases thousands of oxygenating molecules and negative ions into the air and your environment."[72] "Negative ions clear the air of mold spores, pollen, pet dander, odors, cigarette smoke, bacteria, viruses, dust, and other hazardous airborne particles."[73]

The scents are uplifting and good for you. That's a win/win. These plant extracts support health and well-being. High-quality extractions are a wonderful, natural remedy for everything from "clean" home cleaning to calming down or waking up. Aromatherapy is a wonderful complement to other holistic modalities. There are several ways to dispense the essential oils listed below, but if you really want to put the om in the home, I recommend using a diffuser.

Inhalation

Place a few drops in the warmed palm of your hands or a tissue and breathe deeply for personal use. Adding a few drops of essential oil to water in a diffuser is the best vehicle for home use when you want to disperse a scent into the air in a large space.

Topical

You can also apply scent topically, but keep in mind, essential oils are very concentrated. Placing the oil directly on your body speeds up the activation for the desired outcome, but be sure to test it first. Oils are a good alternative to medication for headaches, migraines, muscle soreness, and anxiety. If you have a pet, be sure that the essential oil is either removed from your hands before you touch them or is not toxic to the animal.

Please note: The advice on this page is not intended to replace professional medical help. These statements are for educational purposes only. They are not meant to diagnose, treat, cure, or prevent any illness or disease. This information is offered as a way to use essential oils to assist the body in its own natural processes of reaching balance and homeostasis.

Buyer beware. Do the research and make sure you are buying a quality product with no synthetic fillers or contaminants. Not all oils are made for internal use.

Aromatherapy oils are also good for making cleaning supplies, treating the common cold, regulating hormones, bathing, making massage oils, and creating your own personal lotions, scents, and even bug repellents.[74] To create any of these products, there must be a carrier oil, liquid, or lotion to dilute and apply the oil.[75]

Is there anything an essential oil can't do? Choose the right scent for the job, and your options are limitless. Essential oils are pure and can be very potent. A little goes a long way—you need just a couple of drops.

Learning what type of essential oil is right for you can be an education unto itself. It's something to keep in mind because the information can be overwhelming.

> Florals are calming (rose, lavender, ylang-ylang).
>
> Mints are activating (peppermint, spearmint, rosemary).
>
> Citrus is cleansing and uplifting (lemon, lime, orange, bergamot).
>
> Woods and barks are grounding (frankincense, sandalwood, palo santo, vetiver).

Here are some suggestions for scents in a space:

Kitchen

Any citrus scent. These scents have antifungal and antibacterial properties that make them ideal for cleaning solutions as well as natural disinfectants. Spicy scents are nice in the winter and around the holidays.

Living Room

To reduce stress/negativity:

Bergamot, rose, frankincense, lavender, ylang-ylang, geranium, orange, sandalwood, chamomile, vetiver

To energize:

Rosemary, basil, peppermint, cedar, vetiver, grapefruit, pine, juniper, rosemary, spearmint, jasmine

To clear negative energy:

Sage oil, peppermint, frankincense, grapefruit, orange

Bedroom

To rest, reduce stress, relax:

Lavender, vetiver, patchouli, sandalwood, ylang-ylang, chamomile, neroli, marjoram

Home office

To increase energy, stimulate your mind:

Rosemary, jumpier, lemongrass, orange

Universally outstanding scents that do double duty for your body as well as your home:

- Lavender is great for bathing, as is mineral salt. Lavender counteracts negative energy and promotes spiritual growth. It is commonly thought of as the most calming oil.

- Frankincense is considered the king of oils. It supports health, lifts mood, and soothes the body and mind.

- Tea tree oil cleans the skin as well as household surfaces. It relieves minor aches and pains and promotes positivity.

- Lemon will lift your spirits and lift dirt from surfaces. It can calm the mind as quickly as it can energize it. It helps promote weight loss and digestion. Its antifungal and antibacterial properties make it a standout as a fruit, an oil, or a cleanser.

Essential oils should be of high quality. Look for cold-extracted, 100 percent pure plant oils. Only use pure plant compounds. Avoid oils that have been diluted with synthetic fragrances, chemicals, or oils. It is not out of the question to mix a few drops of different oils and come up with a custom combination that suits you—but take a less-is-more approach.

Creating a daily practice of self-care and learning to set and honor boundaries can be supported with the use of essential oils. Scents connect us to nature, intention, and are grounding, which we know has an immediate physiological benefit. There are many, many ways to clear negative energy. One is not objectively better than the others. What's best for you is what works for you.

Crystals

I have always loved crystals. Before I understood their healing properties, I just thought they were beautiful: Mother Nature's perfect jewels. I have a rather spiritual friend, Teddi. I was attracted to her largely for that reason. It was not a surprise that when I was invited to her home for the first time and stood in her living room, I turned to see a large bowl of assorted crystals and geodes; shimmering sun was dancing off the facets of amethyst, celestite, and quartz in the center of her cocktail table. I did not yet realize the full effect crystals have on our personal energy as well as the ability to transform the energy in our living space.

My girlfriend explained to me that a shaman she had met in Peru placed crystals in the center of the table to bring about the equilibrium necessary for healing. So, she followed suit. Teddi told me they make her feel grounded and balanced. She likes that they infuse her home with positive energy and removes negative energy. She told me about their healing properties, as she experiences them, and how to use them. She uses her crystal collection for everything from balancing her chakras to balancing the quality of her drinking water. Teddi became so taken with them, she felt called to create jewelry and trinket boxes, topping each with a stone set with intention. My girlfriend's inner and outer environments are truly aligned.

Mother Nature has been busy at work forming these magnificent gems for millions of years. Having them around us is a perfect way to connect to our deeper selves, nature, and the earth. The process of crystal forming is called crystallization. Most minerals occur naturally as crystals, which often form in nature when liquids cool and start to harden. A crystal's structure is characterized by atoms, ions, or molecules arranged and fitting together in a periodic pattern.

Crystals are as decorative as they are powerful; a perfect conduit for the transmission of good vibes on any kind of healing journey. They generate, radiate, retain, and transfer energy. They hold a stable energy, which is a powerful energy. Powerful energy has the ability to influence the energy around it.

Crystals have been used in the healing arts for centuries. The word crystal comes from the Greek word *krystallos* for ice.[76]

Impurities in the atomic structure of crystals produce their color. Quartz, for example, is normally colorless, but we know it occurs in a range of colors from pink to brown and to the deep purple of amethyst, depending on the number and type of impurities in the structure.

Just being in the presence of a beautiful crystal reminds us to slow down, breathe and become still to gain inner peace.

Crystal therapies cross the boundaries of religious, spiritual, and alternative beliefs. They have become more mainstream as we understand the science behind their energetic properties. We have energy as they have energy. Crystals help unblock, guide, balance, and direct energy where it is most needed. The different properties of crystals are meant to align with areas in need of support or that are weakened physically, emotionally, or spiritually.

Long before any of us were here on Earth to discover this, the Earth had laid the groundwork for such a discovery. Each crystal has a unique structure and impact. Crystals help calm and ground you. They encourage self-esteem, self-expression, and inspire a sense of calm.

They connect you to nature and yourself. They have a wabi-sabi perfection in the imperfect, beauty that is unmatched. It's easy to be overwhelmed when you begin to look at crystals as there is a seemingly endless variety of minerals, crystals, geodes, and semi-precious stones in all sizes and shapes. There are sold as points, pyramids, tumbled stones, natural stones, chunks, clusters, cubes, spheres, hearts, crystals on stands, crystals carved into shapes, crystals to recharge other crystals. There are a lot of choices! I would say to you just trust your intuition and choose whatever speaks to you. It is not uncommon to have one or two types of crystals "call" to you above all others at any given time.

Would you love a big hunk of amethyst or clear quartz in your living space to generally amp up the good vibes, or would you prefer carrying a small round stone with you for health purposes, depending on what your body needs? Some people meditate with crystals. There are as many options as there are goals that we set for ourselves.

For the beginner crystal enthusiast, just play, have fun, do what you feel your mind, body, or spirit most needs in the moment—or simply choose the stone that seems to choose you. We are drawn to what pleases us in life and in crystals.

Placing crystals in your home is a natural extension of putting the om into your home. Think of it as a realignment of energy for your living space (both internally and externally). Be mindful that the creation of your sacred, nourishing space—infused with good energy and deep meaning—is your highest priority. Different crystals emote or absorb different energy, so you want to choose what serves you best. There are several high-vibe crystals that work especially well in areas that you want to energize. Those crystals promote calming energy for areas that are naturally peaceful, such as an office or bedroom. However, if you love it, it works.

Clear Quartz

Clear quartz is the mother of all crystals. It is universally powerful. This is the place to start if you want a good, general, multi-tasking crystal. It also amplifies and magnifies other crystals that are placed near it. Start here to be crystal clear.

Properties: Quartz is clarifying and manifesting. It removes body blocks and clears you of mind, body, spirit clutter.

Where to place: In the bathroom, near the tub as you wash away the day; family room, workspace; any room where you want to be reminded to align with your higher self.

Amethyst

Amethyst runs a close second to clear quartz if you are a beginner crystal enthusiast.

Properties: Once called "a gem on fire," amethyst is a beautiful purple and part of the quartz family. It relaxes; it quiets the mind; it is spiritually healing and offers intuition, abundance, and universally good vibes. It is representative of spirituality, contentment, and connection. It connects you to inner peace.

Where to place: Anywhere, but avoid direct sunlight as the color will fade. It is a fire element. Its energy is heat, passion, action, emotions. It is traditionally associated with the south area of a home or room and with the fame and reputation area of your dwelling. Use its energy to give your life the boost it needs to enhance your standing in the community and within your family. Or place it under your pillow for a great night's sleep.

Aquamarine

Properties: Its name means seawater, and it is light blue in color. It opens lines of communication and encourages spiritual growth. Its fluidity washes away stress and helps you let go of things that no longer serve you. It allows for rejuvenation of the mind, body, and spirit.

Where to place: Place aquamarine in any space that you use for meditation, reflection, or where you need tranquility. It holds water energy. It is traditionally associated with the north area or the career and life path area of the home.

Aventurine

Properties: Aventurine is a green crystal that aids in relaxation, regeneration, and recovery. Consider this your lucky charm. It's great for boosting optimism and enhancing manifestation around finances and career.

Where to place: Place green aventurine in the east or southeast end of a room or home for abundance, vitality, and healthy growth. Place it in your office, on your desk, or anywhere to remind yourself that "you make your own luck."

Black Tourmaline

Properties: Black Tourmaline is cleansing, grounding, and protective. It relieves tension, and is an all-around best negativity-energy cleaner for you and your home.

Where to place: Place black tourmaline at an entrance, windows, at the computer; anywhere you need to feel protected. Black tourmaline is perfect for protecting your home from negative energy. Place a black tourmaline crystal on either side of your front door, preferably outside. You can hide the two crystals in potted plants if you don't want to draw attention to them. Place them on a console, window, or shelf near the door. If you want to cleanse your room because it feels "heavy," place a piece of black tourmaline in each of the four corners.

Blue Lace Agate

Properties: Calming, relaxing, blue lace agate opens communication. It's best for soothing the mind from racing thoughts.

Where to place: Place it in the bedroom or anywhere you want to be reminded to calm down.

Calcite

Properties: Cleansing, nourishing, good for depression. Green calcite promotes good fortune. Orange calcite is like a jolt of vitamin D. Blue calcite for communication.

Where to place: Place it in the kitchen for its "heart of the home" properties or anywhere you need to boost your outlook.

Carnelian

Properties: Boosts confidence, passion, motivation, productivity, energy and is empowering. Carnelian is known as the artist's stone because it encourages creativity.

Where to place: Kitchen, playroom, or game room, anywhere you "get creative." Office or area in your home where you want a productivity push.

Celestite

Properties: Soothing, restorative, calming, peaceful, and grounding.

Where to place: Bedroom; on a night table for a good night's sleep, great for kids' rooms as it's like a visual lullaby.

Citrine

Properties: Abundance, success, and prosperity. Citrine activates imagination, happiness, wealth, and optimism. I once heard that if you carry a piece of citrine in your wallet, you will always feel like you have enough money. Guess who carries citrine in their wallet?

Where to place: Office, kitchen, desk, near money, anywhere you want a reminder to be happy.

Hematite

Properties: Enhances memory, absorbs toxic emotions, and is protective. Hematite helps ground and calm you.

Where to place: Place in the study or office or near the front door, anywhere you want to feel protected.

Malachite

Properties: Transformation, change. Malachite increases balance, abundance, and growth. This stone represents transformation and will help you "turn over a new leaf."

Where to place: Place malachite on a desk or in the family room, anywhere you need a mood stabilizer or a reminder to get in touch with your intention.

Rose Quartz

Properties: Love, self-care, joy, relationships, harmony, and gentle nourishing energy.

Where to place: The bedroom is ideal for rose quartz. Place crystals on the floor surrounding your bed to envelope you in goodness. Place in the bathroom to remind you to take care of yourself.

Pyrite

Properties: "Fool's gold," pyrite represents wealth, abundance, motivation. It opens opportunity and harnesses the Earth's energy.

Where to place: Place it on a desk, in an office, anywhere you want to vibrate higher.

Shungite

Properties: Neutralizes man-made electromagnetic fields (EMF), or radiation, that our electronic devices emit. Purification and detoxification.

Where to place: Place near or on electronic devices such as a computer. Use in an office or in the corners of a room for added grounding and protection.

Selenite

Properties: General healing, calming, purification, relax ation, and restful sleep. Also dispels negative energy. This stone lifts you up. Selenite is a super-cleanser for generally heavy or stagnant energy. It has the unique ability to charge your personal energy as well as that of your environment and other crystals.

Where to place: Use anywhere that you want to clear the energy: bedroom, under the bed, corners of rooms for greater positivity, in darker spaces. Wave it over and around yourself for personal protection.

TAKEAWAYS

- Everything is energy.

- The goal is to have a positive flow of energy or chi. Rid your home of anything that creates blockages or that im- pedes the sense of abundance and spaciousness.

- Strive for balance, the yin and the yang.

- Homes hold energy as people hold energy, as objects hold energy.

- Space clearing is an ancient ritual that cleanses or shifts energy.

- Smudging, essential oils, and crystals are a few of the tools you can use to help shift energy from negative to positive.

9

WHAT'S WIND AND WATER GOT TO DO WITH IT?

One eye sees, the other feels.
— Paul Klee

INCORPORATING FENG SHUI PRINCIPLES INTO your home provides one of the most profound ways to alter the energy on your holistic journey toward living your best life. The disciplines of feng shui and interior design naturally go hand in hand, but just altering your space with feng shui can have an immense impact on creating a better energetic balance.

Feng shui is an ancient metaphysical art practiced by the Chinese for centuries. It is the art of placement and is a scientific discipline based on the analysis of energy within your environment.

This wisdom helps you when you want to manifest a happy home that reflects your healthiest, highest, truest self. According to Terah

Kathryn Collins, founder of the Western School of Feng Shui, "You and your home share a living partnership. Together you can create the physical spaces that hold your vitality and happiness in place."[77]

You want to consciously set intentions and create spaces that are optimal for energy flow, and that will allow you to live in alignment with inner peace, passion, purpose, and fulfillment.

Feng, meaning "wind," and shui, meaning "water," are two of Earth's flowing elements.[78] Just as blood, oxygen, and nutrients flow through the body, energy, or chi, must flow freely and uninhibitedly throughout your environment.

The practice of feng shui helps people establish a better life for themselves, shifting their life perspectives, providing guidance for making better choices as opportunities present themselves. It is also known to assist in shifting habits, behaviors, emotions, and mindsets for the better, promoting a lifestyle change.

According to the teachings of the Yun Lin Temple in Berkeley, California: "Feng Shui deals with the close relationship between one's well-being and his living and working environments. The knowledge of feng shui is actually the study of how to eliminate harmful impacts on one's life from the environments, and how to optimize one's life by acquiring comfort and happiness from the environments."[79]

Feng shui is based on the belief that everything is interconnected, just as in holistic health or the design of a holistic home. Our bodies, lives, thoughts, finances, and relationships are woven together and influenced by the frequency with which we vibrate. These things are integral parts of the conversation because feng shui emphasizes and reconfirms the interconnectedness of all things. It's all about balance, baby.

The thread that binds everything together is energy. How we behave in our home and with our home is surely an important part of that conversation, just as much as how we speak to ourselves or treat our bodies. We are always looking for the harmony in a space and want to "flow" from a place of joy. Things are put in place with intention. This is a practice of intention, not perfection. Let go of any expectation.

Be cognizant that every room, every piece of furniture, every accessory should be there for a reason. The furnishings also carry an energy and should instill the energy of calmness, happiness, completion. The natural extension of home decor and feng shui—to achieve harmony, abundance, wealth, and health—is synergistic. Each element, as in music, is part of a symphony. When I listen to certain music, I am moved. I feel it in my soul. Why shouldn't your home make you feel the same way? A calming sanctuary touches your emotions. You don't have to be moved to tears, but you should have a positive experience, be awakened, or be warmed by the knowledge that this is possible and completely within your control.

I was invited to someone's home in California not long ago, and I commented on how good the home and its surrounding outdoor spaces felt. It had a peaceful, grounding energy to it. I immediately felt relaxed. There were obvious signs that feng shui had been employed.

Beautiful crystals were placed around the home, and a wood-carved Buddha greeted me as I approached the entrance. That told me the homeowners were spiritual, but the harmony within the space was palpable. I asked about feng shui, and of course, the belief was acknowledged: in fact, the owners had had a feng shui grandmaster assess their space. This made such an impression on me. You feel different when feng shui is applied successfully. I carried that feeling from their home with me for months.

There are several "schools" of feng shui. The classical school uses a compass and takes cardinal direction into consideration, while the Black Sect Tantric Buddhist School of Feng Shui is more simplified and better suited for a Western mindset. For the purpose of this book, I am illustrating the Black Sect Tantric Buddhism method of feng shui or BTB.

You may be surprised to learn that you have unconsciously been practicing feng shui already. Some of us have natural intuition when it comes to owning our space and making it feel really good. You probably have incorporated a few modern techniques without even realizing it.

The orientation of a space determines how energy moves through it, with some arrangements being more favorable and others blocking the healthy flow of energy, or chi. You always want to be mindful of the movement around and through your environment.

According to the BTB Feng Shui School: "By understanding the environment as a perfect expression of our spiritual and psychological states, we can use the juncture of self and home, place and being to create true comfort and joy."[80]

I've learned that masters orally passed on their techniques to selected students or relatives from generation to generation until they began to write it down. The basics begin with the understanding that chi, the flow of energy, can affect your living space and, therefore, your life, and therefore your well-being.

If everything carries energy, so too does the layout of your home, furniture, the colors you choose, ornamentation, and artifacts. Everything you choose to put into your home carries an energy field, and each must work together and with you. It is a grounding practice as well. It helps ground you to yourself and the here and now:

the present. You are the living embodiment of the thoughts, beliefs, and emotions that keep everything in tune (or out of tune). Want to feel less harried? Feeling a little lovelorn? Looking for a little more wealth? There's an energetic element for each of those.

Feng shui basics begin with the five elements: The five element theory is generated by the interaction between yin and yang. These interactions provide energies that, according to Taoist cosmology, "are energetic building blocks of all physical matter in the Universe."[81]

THE FIVE ELEMENT THEORY

Wood   Fire   Earth   Metal   Water

Let's break them down:

Each of the five elements has corresponding attributes that it represents.[82] These include energetic qualities, colors, shapes, and materials that can be used to represent the element.

Wood—yang—growth, vitality, abundance, health, prosperity, adaptability

Colors: Greens, browns

Shape: rectangle

Represented by: anything derived from wood: furniture, accessories, building materials, books, wicker, plants, plant-based cloth, plants represented in and on things such as floral wallpaper and textiles, images depicting nature, or lush landscape

Fire—yang—boldness, leadership, success, passion, vitality, transformation. It's wonderful for attraction but beware of too much fire.

Colors: reds, oranges, yellows, purples, magentas

Shapes: triangle, star

Represented by: anything electrical or any kind of lighting: lamps, fires, candles, sunlight; wildlife and things derived from wildlife: leather, feathers, bone, shells, fur; images that depict any of the above as well as people and/or animals and birds

Earth—yin/yang in perfect harmony—stability, balance, grounding, sustainability. It adds a feeling of comfort and safety.

Colors: browns, beiges, sepia tones, yellow, deep orange, muted colors

Shapes: square, rectangle

Represented by: stone, earthenware, ceramics, crystals, Zen items including singing bowls, a Buddha, cairn sculpture, lotus flowers, bonsai plants; images depicting "earthy" landscapes

Metal—yin—clarity, focus, productivity, intellectual intelligence, calm

Colors: whites, metallics, pastels

Shapes: round, oval

Represented by: anything derived from metal, metallic objects, crystals, gemstones, rocks, marble

Water—yin—purity, inner development, abundance, renewal

Color: dark blues, black, dark gray

Shapes: curves, waves

Represented by: mirrors, glass, water features such as fountains, fish tanks

Using these base guiding principles allows you to control the art of placement. When you feel like something is "off-kilter," look to the balance of the elements in your space. What I love about this is the feeling of control it gives you. You may have too much of one or two elements, and you need to add or subtract something to keep the chi in balance. Remember, chi is another name for energy.

Working to balance these five elements properly in your home creates a harmonious environment. Think of the elements as friends; you want them to play nicely with each other. They support each other and lift each other up, complimenting each other's superpowers. This is considered the creative or productive cycle. Think of it as good chi being created. Everyone on the playground is getting along.

The Five Element Cycle

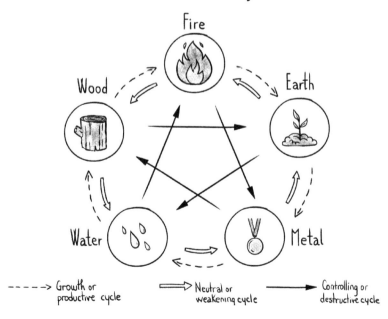

Fire

Wood

Earth

Water

Metal

- - - -> Growth or productive cycle   ⟹ Neutral or weakening cycle   ⟶ Controlling or destructive cycle

The Growth Cycle

Each of the five elements[83] should sustain and nourish one another to create the best balance. I have also heard this described as the generation cycle, the construction cycle, and the creative cycle.[83] Think of it as a parent/child relationship. One element gives birth to or nourishes another. In the illustration, the broken arrows moving clockwise are ideal for showing you how each element enhances another. This cycle promotes growth and expansion.

Fire strengthens Earth—Fire, after burning wood, creates earth by returning to the earth in the form of ash.

> Earth strengthens Metal—Earth is where metal can be found. Minerals are mined from the soil.
>
> Metal strengthens Water—When metal is heated and cooled, water is captured in the air in the form of condensation.
>
> Water strengthens Wood—Water is needed for plants to grow.
>
> Wood strengthens Fire—Wood is needed to feed the fire.[84]

The Neutral or Weakening Cycle

In the illustration, the inner, counter-clockwise, or hollow arrows depict the neutral or weakening cycle. Known as the draining cycle or child-parent cycle, this illustrates how one element weakens or neutralizes the other.[85] When they are at odds with one another, tension may erupt, the elements' powers are diminished, and discord may manifest. But reconstruction can occur.

This neutral or weakening cycle has the power to correct elements that are overwhelming a space and creating imbalances. Detrimental chi is being created when disharmony occurs. Think of it as if you and that group of friends are more like frenemies. You spend time with them, but you know they don't support you the way you would like and that you feel you deserve. You decide you are worth more than that and are going to take matters into your own hands by placing yourself in a more emotionally healthy environment. This cycle is at first depleting, but it can become restorative with awareness.

> Fire weakens Wood—Fire destroys wood.
>
> Wood weakens Water—Wood absorbs water.
>
> Water weakens Metal—Rust forms.
>
> Metal weakens Earth—To mine for metal you must dig up earth.
>
> Earth weakens Fire—Placing earth on fire extinguishes it.

The Controlling or Destructive Cycle[86]

Also known as the grandparent-child relationship, the controlling or destructive cycle is a definite no-no. You want to avoid this inharmonious state among elements. The solid arrows shown in the middle of the diagram are the destructive ones and should be avoided! They even look destructive, don't they?

Think of it as if your playground buddies were aggressively fighting with each other. There is hair pulling and knock-down-drag-out fighting. Tears and trauma may ensure, metaphorically speaking.

> Fire melts metal.
> Metal cuts wood.
> Wood weakens earth.
> Earth weakens water.
> Water puts out fire.

This cycle is interesting. At first glance, yes, it can be seen as abrupt and harmful. However, if you consider these elemental dynamics when carefully adjusted, they could offer order out of chaos to allow for a rebalancing of the elements in a unique way.

For example, let's say you pour water directly on a fire. Naturally, that will trigger a stark reaction. However, think about what happens when you choose to combine fire and water for healing purposes, such as within natural hot springs or inside a sauna. These are great tangible examples of how two opposing elements (fire and water) could work together in creating something new.

Another example is fire melting metal. If the temperature is too hot, it will burn straight through the metal, destroying it. However, if the temperature is just right for that particular metal, it could be shaped, molded, and formed into whatever you wish; something useful or beautiful.

Note that feng shui and the principles that accompany it are never black and white. There is always plenty of room for breathable interactions with the alchemy of transformation.

I have given you examples of home design elements that you can use to incorporate any of the five elements into your decor. Keep in mind that some things like pillows, rugs, decorative accessories, art, and photographs can universally achieve the same thing. You just have to be mindful of which color or material represents which element you want to use and the placement of the element. Here's where I would say: "Listen to your intuition." It always seems to guide you where you need to go.

The Bagua Map

Another tool in the feng shui toolkit is the bagua map.[87] The map—

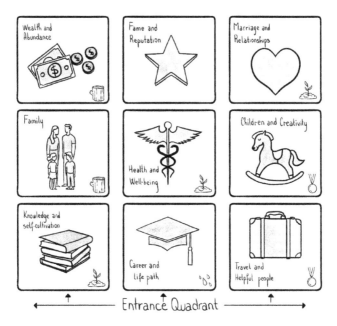

Wealth and Abundance	Fame and Reputation	Marriage and Relationships
Family	Health and Well-being	Children and Creativity
Knowledge and self-cultivation	Career and Life path	Travel and Helpful people

Entrance Quadrant

an energy map or grid—is an easy visual reference that divides a dwelling into "Eight Trigrams." I refer to them as quadrants, or "guas," which is the feng shui term.

The eight trigrams illustrated above reflect nine life areas of your home and correspond to specific areas of your life or "life aspirations." (Although the number of trigrams is eight, we view the life areas as divided into nine sectors because health and well-being are always at the center of them all.) This is our inner core. From our inner core, everything moves outward. From the outward field, everything moves inward: as in feng shui as in life, it's a dance.

The simplicity of this system makes it popular, especially in the West. The map shows that the power of the positive mind is an essential part of life. Aim for easy. You can always make things more complicated, but why?

For years, I had goldfish swimming in a decorative fishbowl on my kitchen counter. The boys, as I called them, were in my health sector, the middle of my home where a part of my kitchen resides on the bagua map. The water in the bowl is considered a water element, for obvious reasons. It helped balance out all the metal of the appliances because water weakens metal. But eventually, after 25 years, my fish died —I kid you not—it wasn't long after that extended period of their healthy lives that I became ill. Coincidence? Who's to say, but I didn't feel well and, in an effort to take back some control, I replaced the fishbowl with a flowering lily plant.

The wood element of the plant is good for health as well as being a great air purifier, but not great overall in the room according to the five-element principle, so I put it in an earthenware pot to better balance the chi. There is always something you can do in the name of balance and harmony. The lily plant is pretty to look at, good for overall well-being, *and* I feel better. That's really all that matters. There is much to be said for feeling like you have some control, and if it's a placebo effect, so be it.

The Black Sect Tantric Buddhist School of Feng Shui accommodates Western culture and modern sensibilities of design. It takes a holistic approach, marrying ancient wisdom with our contemporary way of life.

You can drop the bagua map as if it were an overlay over a floor plan of your whole home, a room in your home, or a specific area like a desk or kitchen counter. It is an essential part of Black Sect Feng shui.

This type of feng shui is a perfect place to start as it has been developed to be easily accessible and employable for even a feng shui novice. You can begin generating better energy and empowering your lifestyle right away.

Returning to the bagua, you will need a floor plan to begin. Super easy tip: place a bagua map on tracing paper the size of your floor plan and overlay it on top of your floor plan, aligning the bagua map to your front door. The door will always fall within one of the three lower quadrants: knowledge and self-cultivation, career and life path, or travel and helpful people.

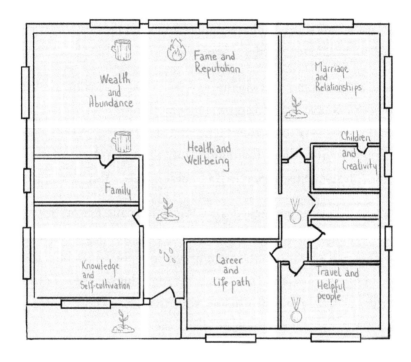

This illustration represents a bagua map overlaid on a floor plan. You can now easily see which energy gua falls where within a home.

Think about each room of your home as a whole, or think about one room at a time, as you lay your bagua map on top of the area you are addressing. Decipher the improvements you would like to see in your life and identify the corresponding area, then study the elements and their relationship to one another to see if you can adjust the environment to suit your specific intention, keeping in mind colors, shapes, and materials that best support the various bagua map areas. Check to see that the elements are activated and balanced to mitigate any destructive outcome. Be aware of any changes in the energy around you.

Have any meaningful coincidences happened? Your awareness, now that it has been sharpened, will see the synchronicity or signs that cannot easily be explained away. This is similar to those occasions when we might think about someone, and then they call, or we run into them accidentally. That is synchronicity.

This all might sound overwhelming, but it's not. Use your intuition. If something looks off or feels off, try something else. There is always more than one way to go about feng shui-ing a space. Just try a small tweak and go from there. Remember, too, this is another tool in your toolkit. Choose to use it or choose something else. You have options.

My client Maggie approached me about improving her outdoor living space and helping her interject more of her personality within it. The long, narrow patio in the front of her home was made that much more important because you passed through the space to get to the front door. This whole area shapes your first impression, and it was lackluster. Maggie is anything but lackluster!

The garden door aligned with her front door in her career and life path gua. To the right, in her travel and helpful people gua, sat a small bistro table and chairs. To the left of the front door, in Maggie's knowledge and self-cultivation gua, resides the living area. I wanted to address the areas from an interior design and feng shui standpoint.

The small eating area's bistro table and chairs are made of metal, so that's great, as that is the favorable element for that gua. It does seem far removed from the living area positioned on the opposite side of the patio. That calls for an earth element, and in the center between both areas, a portable water fountain by the door would be an auspicious addition because it lies in Maggie's career gua, and that calls for a water element. My goal was to tie together each area visually by creating continuity among disparate spaces while activating each gua leading to harmony and well-being.

We did that with matching colorful royal blue cushions for the dining chairs and love seat and loungers in the living area. Then we added pillows in different hues of gray. Now the two seating areas spoke the same color language, and a love connection was made.

There was also an unsightly, exposed central air conditioning unit that needed to be hidden: a screen of bamboo tied together would do nicely. Plants in pots of varying heights on the left side of the patio brought more good energy in the form of the earth element. Stringing lights above the area helped draw the eye upward while simultaneously bringing in the fire element and making the area feel more spacious, sparkly, and intimate.

A multicolored outdoor area rug defined and grounded the outdoor living room area. I suggested a pale terra-cotta paint color for the gate door, from which Maggie hung a darker terra-cotta sun sculpture that had been resting on the ground. It added another layer of interest in the outdoor space, as well as when looking through the windows from the inside. That was just the dash of drama the space needed to look more inviting and restricted energy from going right out the gate.

With the plants, flowers, cushions, and new paint, all elements were represented, balanced, and beautiful. Incorporating feng shui and interior design principles took the space from drab to fab!

It had a huge impact on the way Maggie uses the space and feels in the space. This once-neglected "in-between" area is now a place for entertaining and has prompted a newly adopted horticultural hobby. It opened a door to curiosity, and community Maggie had not known in a while. She relayed to me how happy she felt, and she plans to incorporate feng shui techniques in a bigger way moving forward.

If your intention is to strengthen friendships or create a larger sense of community, find that area on the bagua map that speaks to people and connection. That is an earth element. Earth elements are represented in shades of brown and sepia. A square is the earth shape. Fire strengthens earth so maybe incorporating those reds and pinks is a good idea for upping the energy.

You might want to add a photo of friends—the photo being of rectangular shape—or a collection of things you are passionate about that you would like to share with others: something representing a trip outdoors, such as a ski or camping trip, bird watching, or white-water rafting. A caveat: if the relationship sector falls in your bedroom, I would stay away from inviting in more people. This is a case where I would look to another area in the house to utilize these principles.

If you want to strengthen relationships, you could also look to the helpful people. For example, maybe you belong to a travel club with friends or want to share your life with like-minded people. Helpful people and travel are represented by the metal element. How could you incorporate more of that—or a representative of that—into the room that the bagua map indicates as being for helpful people and travel as a sector? For example, in my house, it would be in the living room at the front of the house.

Looking at your health and well-being area would not be out of the question either, because friendships and a sense of community create unity and are so integral for our overall well-being. I would not consider the love and relationship sector of your home. That is reserved for more intimate relationships. Simply look at the area you want to boost: choose a color or material, or element that corresponds and find a way to incorporate it into your living space in a way that speaks to you.

In traditional feng shui, the idea was to use design elements such as nine lemons in a bowl for good luck and vibrant energy, or six coins in a fountain for wealth and abundance, among other things. That makes no sense to me personally and doesn't align with my lifestyle. Incorporating a gold or silver object representing metal or a beautiful piece of artwork representing water, that makes sense to me. Modern feng shui should match your lifestyle and symbolic language.

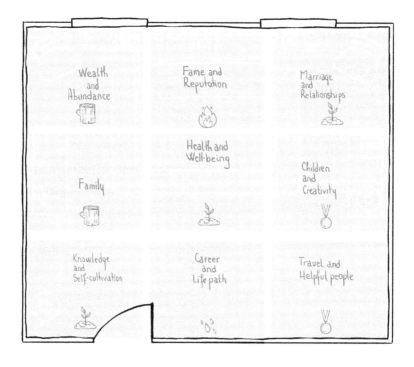

I am often asked about how to make a bedroom more attractive and romantic. The master bedroom is one of the most important rooms in feng shui. Therefore, what you do with, and in your master bedroom has far-reaching implications for your well-being, harmony, and relationships. It should be a haven of intimacy and solace. It should be a place to unwind, a place for romance and rest.

Does your bedroom provide for all of that? Is it a cozy nest, a rejuvenating sensual oasis? Is it peaceful, quiet, and conducive to long deep sleep? How your bedroom makes you feel makes all the difference.

After we lay our bagua map over the bedroom floor plan, we can begin. I would start with a wooden headboard in the command position. If you have an upholstered headboard, it most likely has a wood frame which is okay. It makes you feel supported and grounded.

Make your bed every day. It is good for the soul and easily creates a feeling of accomplishment right from the get-go; your bedroom immediately looks neater.

Is your room made for two if there are two of you? Are you both represented? Or, if you are single and want to call in a partner, have you made room for one? Are there pairs of things?

Is there anything over your bed that has a heaviness, is angular, or represents singularity, such as art, a fan, or beams? These would be a no-no. You don't want beams or a fan, at least directly over the bed, because they appear to be cutting, which is divisive.

Make sure nothing is hiding under the bed or in drawers that does not connote a fresh start with an open heart. It's energy, after all. Remember, just because we can't see it, doesn't mean energy is not lingering there: letters from a past love, wills, and divorce documents (I've seen it!), clothes under the bed that do not represent you presently. These are threads tying you to unwanted energy. Family photos or pictures of groups of people facing the bed are a no-no too. You do not want to call more people into the bedroom.

Remember, you don't want to activate this quiet and restorative place, no matter where it falls on your bagua map. But you can punch up the romantic aspects with colors and/or symbols in accordance with feng shui principles. For example, let's suppose your bedroom is in the front of your house, in your helpful people sector when you lay your bagua map over your floor plan. You could now look at the element signifying that area—metal— and incorporate it by adding something like a photo of you and your spouse in a gold metal frame. Use white as the primary color on your walls, and consider if the wood element, the productive element, might be used to "bump up" the metal element. Colors and shapes all bolster the metal. I always add some rose quartz to the bedroom. The bedroom is yin energy, honor that.

A universal intention for many people is to call forth more money. Money is energy, and your thoughts around it create your reality or story about it. If you think you have enough money, you do, and you feel abundant. If you are coming from a place of lack, there will never be enough. In the case of the latter, you must start by clearing up any limiting beliefs around money, then perhaps incorporate some feng shui tools to heighten the vibration of abundance and wealth. We would look at the upper left sector—wealth and prosperity—to do this. You might also want to look at the bottom center quadrant, your career gua, because if we advance in our career, it will show up as more money in our pockets.

Reference these areas on your bagua map and examine where they fall within your home. Then choose how you want to proceed. For example, if your wealth area falls in the kitchen and the wealth element is wood, wood connotes growth, vitality, abundance, health, prosperity. Think about placing something representing wood in that area. Water strengthens wood and helps increase its flow, so a water element would also be appropriate. A plant potted in a wicker container is a perfect choice. I might add a few coins into the soil for a "money boost." Also representing wealth are the colors purple, blue, and red. How might you incorporate them? Consider flowers in any or all of those colors.

Perhaps another way to feng shui around the intention of more money is to feng shui your desktop or any quadrant in your home where you're working with your finances.

Lay your bagua map over the drawing of your desk. Now your wealth corner is at the top left-hand side of the desk. Could you put a plant there? Jade is perfect as it is "a money tree, something green for growth or blue for wealth? A collection of books, or an object that signifies "you made it," is also good.

This is a very basic explanation of feng shui just to provide you with a sense of how the role of the elements influence each other within your space.

Begin to work with these concepts studying how they might "play together" to strengthen the yin and the yang balance for harmony in your home or office. Modern feng shui has a pragmatism to it. There are some universal truths in feng shui, and there are small tweaks you can incorporate today to improve the flow in your home. Lean in and feel the shift.

Here are what I consider feng shui basics:

1. Arrange your furniture in a command position—meaning that you want to see the door, but not be directly in line with the door—from your sofa, bed, favorite chair. You see the entry point. You see who's coming and going. This allows you to be "in command" of the energy flowing into the room. You never want your back to the door or main entrance and exit point.

2. Clear the clutter! Good chi favors cleanliness and organiza-

tion first and foremost.

3. Plants are always a good idea. They are considered auspicious. Plants in a wealth corner of a desk or in your health area are perfect. There is some controversy surrounding plants in the bedroom, however. Many experts say it's fine, but some feel it's too energizing. Plants are a wood element, and that is considered activating. They also need to be watered, so that brings in the water element, which might affect your sleep. Go with your gut. Plants with rounded leaves are preferred over plants with jagged leaves or cacti. The prickly varieties are considered cutting and divisive. Always make sure that plants look at the peak of health.

4. Consider air purifiers, open windows, turning on a fan to circulate energy.

5. Hide or mask electronics, especially in the bedroom.

6. Lighten up. Different kinds of light sources allow you "to see clearly."

7. Remove your shoes when you step through the door. You are keeping the outside outside.

8. Your entrance is the "mouth of the house." This is where the chi enters. Keep it clean and clear. The outside should also be clean and clear of any debris. Paths, lights, perhaps container gardens, keep them all immaculate.

9. Your windows are the "eyes" of the home. Keep them clean as well. The better to see you with. Proper window coverings, when necessary, allows you to control the flow of energy. I love soft filtered light when it's very bright outside. At night, you ideally want to close curtains or blinds

to cover the big, dark rectangles that bring with them too much yang energy. One of my daily rituals, which gives me a surprising amount of joy, is opening my blinds every morning and flooding my room with light. I look past my house at the view and take a moment to practice gratitude for the new day.

10. Remove any negative or violent symbolism in art, photographs, book covers, or anything similar from anywhere in view. The implications of violence are not auspicious.

11. Keep bathroom doors shut and toilet lids closed. You don't want to "flush prosperity down the drain."

12. Make sure everything is in good condition, make repairs as necessary.

13. Do not store anything under beds. That traps energy. You can run, but you can't hide.

14. If it doesn't feel right or good, it is not good feng shui for you.

15. There should be nothing above your bed that gives the illusion of "cutting" you. No beams, no heavy fixtures. No metal sculptures, nothing "coming at you."

16. Reflect something beautiful with a mirror to double the positive energy flow. Different schools think about this differently. There are some conflicting opinions about having a mirror directly across from the front door of your home. You are supposedly bouncing energy or fortune right back out the door. There are ways around this, however. Sometimes, especially in a dark, small entry, it might be a welcome sight. The designer in me would instinctively want to bring the reflective surface into the space for more light.

Can you tweak the way it is hung? Can you put something in front of it? Can the mirror hang off to the side for touch-ups on the way out the door? A small console table, plant, or object placed under and in front of it, perhaps? I will say what I always say: "If you love it and it feels right to you, keep it." In your mind, you are still welcoming in goodness and prosperity.

17. Furniture should not be placed flat against a wall. You ideally want space all around the furniture to continue the "good flow." This is especially true for the bed.

18. Pairs of things in a bedroom speak of the couple that resides there. If you are single and you are hoping for a partner, then placing pairs of things is doubly important.

To achieve "good vibes," you want feng shui to support your good thoughts and intentions. You must listen to your intuition and trust yourself. While there are certain hard and fast rules, there are also many different schools of thought. If something doesn't feel right—don't do it. It should always feel easy. You want your body to be relaxed and your mind at ease. This is another opportunity to go within yourself and ask, "How does this make me feel?" In feng shui ,as in life, simplicity is the best policy for reducing stress. I've learned that if things start to appear too complicated, move on.

If interior design is like medicine for the soul and you are consciously creating your best, most authentic self, you'll always do what you know to be best for you.

TAKEAWAYS

• Clearing clutter is step number 1.

• Using feng shui principles is another tool to help improve the energy and harmony in your home.

- Think of modern-day feng shui as rooted in pragmatism and beauty. Follow your intuition.

- Use the five elements to help balance energy and create harmony.

- The perfect balance of yin and yang energy is in the earth element.

- Feng shui rules can be applied to any environment.

- Overlay your bagua map on any area you want to improve. Be sure to align it with your front door.

- You can feng shui your home as a whole, or feng shui one room or one area. It's up to you, based on your goal.

10

FOCUS ON DESIGN

*The best rooms have something to say about the
people who live in them.*
—David Hicks

WHEN IT COMES TO DESIGN, CLIENTS OFTEN TELL
me they don't want a space to feel "too decorated." Your goal is to make
your space not only beautiful but to have it feel lived-in, reflective of
who you are, how you live, and what you love. Bringing all these principles together in a way that injects your personality into the space is defined as your design aesthetic. If you're bubbly and you know it, design
with joie de vivre, using bright colors and a lot of shapes or patterns. If
you are cerebral and seek solitude, maybe a well-stocked library artic-
ulates your love of learning and need for solitude. A more introverted
soul might envelop themselves in muted tones that will create the seren-
ity they seek. Heavy mixed metals may speak to a dynamic personality.
Having said that, if you love something, it works. Finding the right

place for any object is key, but the joy of an object that reflects joy back is far richer than any rule that you could follow.

Beauty is not in the eye of the beholder. "Beauty is in the brain of the beholder." When we experience something, we define as beautiful, and we all experience beauty differently, blood flows to the medial orbitofrontal cortex. That part of the brain lights up like a Christmas tree and stimulates our pleasure center. We associate beauty with love and desire and become attached to what we admire. Blood flows where emotions go.

Rooms void of loved objects may appear soulless. Art is such a profound way to express yourself. One of my favorite things to do when I travel is to find that perfect something for my home: the thing that serves as a happy memory from the trip and adds to the ever-expanding story of my life. Collecting things for your home from far-off places you've traveled is a delightful way to represent who you are and help illustrate your story, as is anything you hold in high esteem.

Think about a time when you were away, perhaps at a resort or hotel you enjoyed, where you felt stress melt away and felt a sense of lightness. Your home should be your own personal retreat that makes you feel relaxed and happy, like that hotel room.

A bedroom should be a warm and welcoming retreat at the end of the day. The desire to bring back the look of a favorite hotel into your own home is big business. What if you could capture and bottle that feeling? What do designers of upscale hospitality spaces know that you don't? Every detail was thought out to make your experience better. Attention to detail and common-sense hacks that make a hotel room feel like an oasis is all it takes. You want to recreate the feeling.

The first thing you may notice is there is never any clutter. The hotel room may feel slightly impersonal, but it's the negative space we feel good about. What you put in a room is as important as what you leave out of a room. Tight, cramped, cluttered spaces make us feel closed in. We want to feel "expanded."

Maybe you weren't able to articulate your feelings at the time, but now you can because you are going to go inward and identify them. Using the mind/body compass we discussed earlier can help you identify these feelings. This is a lesson I have been trying to teach my husband for years. We always "discuss" the choice of hotel options when we are making our travel plans. He believes we are just going somewhere to sleep, so why get crazy about the look and feel of a room. For me, life is too short not to be at peace in a foreign place, and comfort is key when traveling. It enhances my total experience. And that's what "Living beautiFULLY" is all about, making an experience the best it can be.

I don't know about you but give me a fresh, fluffy oversized towel after a great shower with steam, and I'm snug as a bug in a rug. When was the last time you replaced your towels or even your sheets? Steam, wonderful gels, and soaps—yes, please! Little luxuries go a long way toward elevating any experience.

Hotels are clean, the windows clear, maybe the outside is brought in. Fresh plants, flowers, even a bowl of fruit are often in sight. The hospitality industry thinks about wellness and the overall user experience now more than ever. The last time I was in a hotel, they offered me nightly massage oil for my temples and pulse points to help me wind down. Each night by the bed, slippers at the ready and a small piece of chocolate on my pillow, there was a list of my options for the scent of the oil the following night. What a lovely gesture. They were appealing to all my senses. These are no longer little luxuries; they are fundamental for well-being.

Creating your own retreat takes nothing more than a desire and awareness to master a few simple design elements that enhance your interiors and help you achieve that outcome. These things are essential for reducing feelings of stress in a room and creating a sense of overall well-being.

One of the first questions I always ask my clients is: "Do you have a design style?" I am looking for clues to their aesthetic if one has not already been well defined. I am often met with a look of confusion. The "I don't know" look. But you most likely do know; you just didn't think about it. We all have predilections toward some things more than others. It really comes down to knowing yourself and how you like to live. When you're able to identify what makes your heart sing and what hits a sour note, that's YOU.

I often say, "It's as important to know what you don't like as what you do like." Your inner knowing will always move you in the right direction, but you must pay attention.

What is your design style?

Some key things to think about:

1. What does your living space look like presently? What do you like or dislike?

2. What do you naturally gravitate toward in terms of color, texture, overall look, and style?

3. What personality traits would you describe yourself as having? Would they have a color or style preference?

4. How would you describe your personality? How would others describe you? Are you bubbly and colorful, or do you lean toward introspective and cerebral?

5. Would you say you are more a minimalist or a maximalist?

6. What do you value?

7. Are you more of a do-it-yourselfer, a do-it-for-less person, or a do-it-all-over type?

8. What area do you live in? Location and weather should be considered when decorating as the inside and the outside coexist.

9. How do you spend most of your time? Are you a bookworm or a binge-watcher? Do you get outdoors often or curl up on the couch?

10. Where did you grow up, and what kinds of things did you grow up surrounded by?

Color and Light

Color has the power to change our mood.[88] Light makes us feel good and is critical to our health and well-being.[89] Nutritious meals are good for our bodies. A practice of gratitude increases happiness and life satisfaction.[90] Everything is energy, and to have good chi, we need balance. Small tweaks we make can have a big impact on our lives.

With all of this in mind, it's important to create a uniquely authentic, well-designed space that reflects your personality and connects to that which nourishes your soul—it all goes hand in hand. Your goal is to create a synergy between your environment and your mind, body, and spirit.

There are many subjective likes and dislikes in interior design—you do you.

Don't be afraid to express your point of view. Add what speaks to you, what you love, and what you know makes you feel your best. Subtract those things that you do not love or are not useful, and you can't go wrong mapping out your design aesthetic, one that reflects you authentically. If you don't know what your design aesthetic is, do what I tell all my clients to do: cut pictures out of magazines, create Pinterest boards, or anything else that allows you to collect information based on what you are attracted to or find beautiful. You don't even necessarily have to know why something makes sense to you in the moment, keep sleuthing, patterns will begin to emerge that will become a little window into your soul.

Balance

In interior design, as in life, balance is key. You need the yin to balance the yang. You need the light to balance the dark. You need the old to balance the new. In interior design, balance is the relationship in size between two or more objects, between design elements, and how each relates to another—such as an element's shape, color, and texture. Balance provides stability and structure to an environment.

Consider questions like these: Does the desk on one side of the bed have the same height and weight as the night table on the opposite side of the bed? Does a small piece of furniture look inadequate next to a big, imposing piece of furniture? Do the lamps coordinate or hold the same visual weight? Many times, you can step back and "eyeball" something and feel if it is right or wrong.

Like Goldilocks and the three bears, you'll know when something is too big or too small. It feels off. You are looking for the sweet spot where the object or grouping is just right. Your intuition will guide you. Sometimes, something may seem counterintuitive, like having big furniture in a small room, but this can work because it makes a small room appear bigger. Mixing metals or wood tones was once thought of as gauche, but now it is commonplace. Trends change, everyone is unique, and design is fluid. Think outside the box and trust yourself. When you know the rules, you can break the rules; do it confidently.

If you find this kind of thing difficult to understand, you may want to call in a professional to help you. It is always worth the money to do something right the first time.

The most common mistake that people make is incorrect proportion.

There are two types of balance:

- **Symmetrical**: One side of a space is the mirror image of the other side. Both sides are evenly balanced with the exact same objects, such as matching chairs on either side of a sofa. This is also the easiest design to achieve. It may give a more formal appearance, but it is a fail-safe for a design novice.

- **Asymmetrical**: Asymmetry is the opposite of symmetry. The visual weight of line, color, form, and shape is balanced without exact duplication. There is no mirror image, but there is more visual interest that creates a more informal look. For example, two chairs are placed on the left of the sofa, and a love seat is placed across from them on the right side of the sofa. A chest and lamp on one side of a doorway and a desk with a mirror on the other side of a doorway is another example. This takes slightly more mastery to pull off. Large objects have more visual weight than small objects; dark colors hold more weight than light colors. If you have one heavy object, you can use multiple small objects for balance. When you've achieved an attractive visual weight, then you've achieved a balance of objects.

Focal Point

This is the visual point of reference to which the eye always returns. It is the first thing viewers see when they enter the room, and it is the point of interest in your layout. It is the star of the show. Everything else is a supporting player. Often there is an obvious focal point such as the largest piece of furniture in a room, the view out the window, interesting architectural details, or a fireplace or built-in wall unit that may "take command."

You could create a focal point with a piece of furniture that makes a statement, wallpapering or painting an accent wall, hanging a bold piece of art. Is there something in the room that is a conversation starter? That would be a focal point because you would naturally be drawn to it. You really want one thing in the room to "grab" your attention, and your eye will naturally gravitate toward it over and over. Place the seating area around it to emphasize the focal point's importance. Highlight the focal point to play up its importance.

As a fun exercise, if you are unfamiliar with focal points in interiors, look through magazines or look at different environments to find the focal point. Notice what your eyes immediately gravitate toward. There may be several focal points. Your eyes should easily move from one thing to the next in a rhythmic way. If there is no place to "rest your eye" or everything seems to be vying for your attention, pay attention to how that makes you feel. Chaos comes from overstimulation. Too many things competing for your attention creates anxiety.

Keep in mind the negative space as well. Objects need room to breathe. Every corner and every surface doesn't need to be filled. Quiet moments are restful moments. We need them to allow other things to shine. Loud, bright, busy things have a tendency to pull your eye to them. Taking a somewhat minimalist approach is always your best bet if you are unsure.

Scale

Scale refers to the overall size of something in relation to another object or a space. Scale usually refers to the size of an object or space in relation to the human body or another element, as well as the size of the space itself. How high are your counters, vanity, or sinks in relationship to your height? Think about the length of your legs when considering the depth of a sofa. How big is the sofa in relation to your room? When an object is too small, and something looks insignificant, it may appear to be swallowed up by what's around it. Too big, and it takes over the space. If you are using several types of patterned textiles in a room, make sure there is a variation in scale from one to the next.

Harmony

Harmony refers to the overall success of blending different elements

together to create a sense of belonging, such as the pairing of furniture or accessories that craft a beautiful vignette. The goal is to
have different elements in the room that complement each other
and are visually connected in some way. Keep this in mind as you
add elements. Size, scale, color, shape, and pattern all come into play,
moving your eye around the room in a harmonious way. Repetition
is helpful here. Repeating elements or colors help create harmony.

Each element is a note that, when strung together, creates a beautiful symphony. This also applies to the harmony and unity between
rooms. You don't want a disjointed look as you move from room to
room. You want a cohesive "theme" to keep that rhythmic symphony
playing throughout the house.

Tension

I believe it's important to create a little tension between objects for a
sophisticated design mix. Not everything has to match. In fact, the
best interiors have divergent elements, but the scale is correct, the
unity is strong, and the space is balanced. Contrast opposites side by
side, such as old and new, rustic and refined, hard and soft, dark and
light. The space is balanced, and that makes for a compelling
narrative.

Lighting

I am a stickler for good, layered lighting. I truly believe this is one of the most underused design principles. You can spend tons of time working on getting the floor plan right, hours upon hours sourcing furniture, and curating the perfect accessories to complement it all, but it means nothing if the light is all wrong! Light levels are as integral to our well-being as any design principle. With the touch of a dimmer switch, we can transform the attitude, mood, or look of a space and our experience in it.

Light also helps us understand time. We have "built-in clocks": these "clocks" are known as our circadian rhythm, shining a light on our body's natural wake/sleep cycle informs our bodily functions and behavior that repeats itself every 24 hours. Morning light cues our body to begin gearing up for the day. Evening light informs our body to begin to unwind.

When it comes to lighting, your circadian rhythm is important to so many aspects of your health, ranging from your metabolism to your mood, brain function, and autoimmune activity.[91]

We want to work *with* our body's natural biological functioning, not against it. Lighting systems or circadian rhythm bulbs follow your 24-hour sleep/wake cycle by signaling alertness during the day and supporting relaxation and sleep at night. They act as our hypothalamus acts to initiate the release of cortisol early in the day and melatonin as the blue light fades and red light is more pronounced.[92] We are cueing our bodies to respond physiologically. The color of the light in circadian rhythm bulbs actually changes. It shifts from cool to warm, brighter blue light during "peak" times and a softer amber light as you are winding down. This helps support sleep which is also so critically important.

High efficiency, warm white light LED bulbs are replacing incandescent bulbs. Fluorescent and incandescent bulbs throw off light in all directions so that you lose 40–50 percent of the light source. LED lights emit light downward. The colors of LED lighting effects our health by helping to regulate biological rhythms. Every cell of our bodies is impacted by this. White light has positive effects during the day, while red light has almost none. Yellow and orange have little.[93] Blue light, however, has the biggest negative impact on regulating circadian rhythm. Disruption of the circadian rhythm occurs especially from backlit technology, and it creates adverse effects on our overall health.[94]

The stimulation provided by light and color has the ability to excite us, depress us, heal us, create harmony, or create disharmony. If you walk into a room with dull fluorescent lights, you tend to want to crawl into a hole. Conversely, if you walk into a well-lit room with light streaming through a window, your mood is uplifted in an instant.

You want to aim for multiple sources of lighting in a room. A room benefits from:

- Ambient or general lighting: This kind of lighting illuminates the entire room. It is the most common lighting in a home. It may come from your windows, or it might be an addition to or in place of any natural light you may be lacking. It is a good, overall, everyday lighting source, but please don't stop there. The most popular general overhead lighting styles are chandeliers, flush mounts, recessed lighting, or track lighting. I would incorporate table lamps or floor lamps for added light and added interest.

- Task lighting: This direct type of lighting casts illumination on an area for a specific task, where you need brighter light. A reading lamp, a desk lamp, vanity lights, lighting over a workstation, or pendants over an island are all great examples of task lighting. A good rule of thumb is that task lighting should not be more than two to three times as bright as ambient light. The task at hand should be really well lit, but you don't want the lighting to be a beacon in the room. You can also fix bad lighting that is casting shadows with additional task lighting.

- Accent lighting: This sets a mood and is also referred to as mood lighting or directional lighting. It can accent art, architectural details such as a niche, the inside of wall units, built-ins, or a bar. Uplighting—lighting that comes from the floor and illuminates upward—makes a perfect accent for a dark corner or to highlight something like a plant or a sculpture. The shadows that this type of lighting can create are as fascinating to look at as the object you are emphasizing. Uplighting is similar to spotlights that focus on something intentional but often illuminate from above.

Ask yourself this question over and over: "What am I trying to emphasize?" How do you want each room to make you feel? What is the purpose or function of the space? Day or night, a room should be inviting.

The following suggestions can help:

- Ideally, all types of lighting should be present in a room: accent, task, and ambient. Keep lighting at different eye levels: this introduces another layer of visual interest. Many types overlap in their functionality, especially if lights are on dimmers, which I highly recommend.

- Entryway: Start with a dramatic flush-mount or chandelier overhead if you have the height. You are putting your best and brightest foot forward.

- Living room: This is a good place to use recessed lighting throughout. If your room has a main seating area, I love a large overhead fixture to center it. Floor lamps are nice for lighting shadowy corners. Lights built into wall units or installed to accent art are a must if your aim is to accentuate your belongings. Table lamps on side tables and/or a reading lamp next to your coziest spot can be as functional as it is beautiful.

- Dining room: The dining room is ideal for dramatic, moody lighting. The main source should come from a chandelier or two centered over the table. I love sconces in this room as well, along with lights on a buffet if applicable.

- Kitchen: Kitchen lighting can prove to be the most complex. You definitely need as much overhead light in the kitchen as makes sense. Task areas like an island and an eat-in area benefit from pendants or additional fixtures. Work areas benefit from the addition of under-cabinet lighting. LED puck lights over the task areas in your kitchen are a must.

- Bedroom: Ideally, bedrooms have a main overhead light source as well as table lamps on nightstands or hanging by the bed. I always add candles to up the romance.

- Bathroom: Recessed lighting is a must, as well as task lighting alongside or above the mirror. I love backlit mirrors or the kind that have the lighting built-in for a streamlined look. A chandelier over a tub has a certain *je ne sais quoi*.

- Office: Start with recessed lighting or a main overhead source. Obviously, use a desk lamp on your desk and any other accents you feel you might like. Treat this room with the importance of each of the other rooms in your home.

This is where you work, possibly making money. You need it to be conducive to productivity and accomplishment.

TAKEAWAYS

- A well-designed environment has the power to promote health, happiness, and well-being.

- Knowing basic design principles provides a fail-safe approach to achieve great results in your living space.

- Start with a plan.

- Use layers of light within each room.

- Following your circadian rhythm within the lighting plan further promotes well-being.

- Know how you will live in the space and what you need this room to provide you with.

- How a room makes you feel depends on the atmosphere you create when imposing your aesthetic.

- Build your room around the natural focal point.

- The focal point refers to how much your eye is attracted to something.

- Consider balance, scale, harmony, texture, and unity in an environment.

- Always be conscious of your feeling-state within a space. Let that be your guide.

11

COLOR MY WORLD

Color is a power which directly influences the soul.
—Wassily Kandinsky

AS MUCH AS LIGHT HAS THE ABILITY TO CHANGE our mood, so too does color. The psychology of color is the study of human behavior as dictated by color or how it affects the mind and impacts our well-being. [95] It is a relatively new field that is closely related to both chromotherapy (color therapy) and phototherapy (light therapy). Think energizing red, sunshine yellow. These are considered warm colors, along with orange. Warm colors evoke emotions ranging from feelings of warmth and comfort to feelings of anger and hostility. Blue, green, or purple are cool colors. These colors are often described as calming but can also call to mind feelings of sadness or indifference. Through color, we express joy and sadness, vivaciousness and melancholy. That's the amazing thing about color. It is extremely communicative, as in a blue mood or feeling green with envy.

Color is more than a visual experience. Different hues, tones, and shades can be cleverly employed to evoke specific feelings and perceptions—influencing decisions and behavior. Color in our home speaks to who we are and what our aesthetic is. The color in decorative or unadorned spaces is a window into our soul.

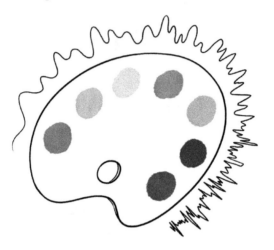

It was Isaac Newton who discovered that when pure light passes through a prism, it separates itself into a range of colors.[96] It was Newton who identified the ROYGBIV color spectrum (red, orange, yellow, green, blue, indigo, violet) that make up a rainbow that can be seen by the human eye. Each color is made up of a single wavelength and cannot be split further into more colors.[97] Hence, every color has its own identity and meaning and thus can be used to influence people in different ways.

The colors we use to decorate our home have a profound effect on our emotional state of being. Color has the power to help us heal as well as the power to harm us. Color can radically affect mood and emotion; some of that response is wired within us. Our brain waves react to color or the energy we perceive each color to exhibit. Examining the different levels of arousal color elicits shows what can be changed with a change in color. Studies reveal that our brainwaves or output of energy change in relationship to color or the mood it evokes in us.[98]

The results can be dramatic because color deeply affects us emotionally, physically, and psychologically, consciously and unconsciously. When I think of yellow, I always think of a smiley face. That colors me happy. Green, in my mind's eye, puts me in nature; blue has me floating, face toward the sun in an ocean, while red stops me in my tracks.

As Pablo Picasso once said, *"Colors, like features, follow the changes of the emotions."*[99]

Color psychology is carefully considered when designing almost anything and says much about each of us. It transforms lives. The idea that colors, especially our favorite colors, are somehow linked to our personalities is also explored in color psychology.[100]

The use of color conveys a lot of meaning depending on context. From the colors in the clothes we wear to the choices in our home's decor, we are communicating much about how we see ourselves and how we want to be seen. Each of us has a color(s) preference. It is not uncommon to naturally gravitate, subconsciously, toward color preferences that are the most flattering for you, even if you are someone who assumes you do not give color much thought. I always rolled my eyes back in the day when "color consultants" would advise based on "what season" you were: winter, spring, summer, or fall. Each had a corresponding color palette you were supposed to stay within, which was so confining.

Don't know what colors you tend to gravitate toward or are most flattering to your eye? Many designers say that when they are getting to know their clients, they will often look into the client's closets to get a sense of their color predilections. Designers theorize that what is hanging in your closet is a sure way to tell what you might like to be enveloped within your home. Are the clothes more neutral or colorful, warm or cool? Color personality assessment tests will theorize that what you may choose to call your favorite color is not necessarily a color you would choose to wear.[101]

That is certainly the case with me. My closet is full of black and white clothes. More often than not, I am wearing black. I am trying to color my world, but I somehow always fall back on my love of the color, or non-color, black. Yet if you perused my home, I'd defy you to find any black in the decor. Maybe a picture frame or a wrought iron accessory exists, but I have no black in my home. I don't know why. I am not attracted to it as a decorative color as others are. Sure, I love the sophistication of a dramatic black and white interior, but when I go inward and ask myself, "How does this environment make me feel?" I feel like it is a little too extreme for me as a potential decorative choice—a little too "black and white."

I much prefer brown in my home and, unapologetically, I have a deep attachment to beige. Yet I wear very little in the brown/beige family. Brown is an earth color in color psychology and a wood element in feng shui. It makes me feel warm and grounded in my home. I feel safe. I love being surrounded by natural elements, but I would hardly call myself an "earthy person." I subscribe to the importance of everyday luxuries, and color in small doses moves me and makes my heart beat a little faster. My mostly black and white wardrobe speaks to the balance I try to create in my every day.

I have learned to ask clients the question, "What color do you enjoy surrounding yourself with?" What colors were you surrounded by as a child? To me, that is a better way to understand your color preferences and serves as the best jumping-off point to begin getting in touch with your design aesthetic. Designers will think this is very controversial! That doesn't mean I won't take a peek into your closet. I may still learn things that help with the design process. Which colors do you naturally gravitate toward? What colors make you feel good?

Each color has a distinct personality. Colors, like personalities, have more than one characteristic. We are complex creatures, and color—and combinations of colors—have a unique complexity as well.

Reactions to color can be subjective but, generally, certain types of colors produce particular responses. We base our color choices on learned responses that come from our culture, our background, childhood, who we associate with, how we feel, and what identity we are conveying. Our interpretations can change from day to day or year to year, but universal associations can be made. If you don't know offhand what colors best describe your personality, see if any of the color descriptions below resonate with you. Which color or colors do you naturally gravitate toward? Try them on to see if the fit is right. Feelings about color are fluid. Our proclivity toward certain colors may change over our lifetimes. Decide if something feels good for where you are in your life right now.

Be aware that light has an impact on the depth of color variation. Be sure to look at color in all different kinds of light around or in a room. There are shadows in corners; some colors look different next to a window or across the room. Will you be experiencing the space in bright natural light, artificial light, or candlelight?

Red is the most intense color, and thus, it can provoke the strongest emotions. Red's meaning is associated with excitement, passion, confidence, boldness, strength, danger, anger, and action. It is the color of sexual energy and physical aggression. It is a take-charge color. Are you driven, adventurous? Red demands our attention. Conversely, it is also a color associated with violence and resentfulness.

But in many cultures, it means good luck. The color red tends to stimulate our appetite, which is why it is so often used in areas of dining or spaces where we gather in groups. A little goes a long way, so an accent wall might be a consideration. Too much red can make us anxious or domineering. Red is also the color of the fame and reputation quadrant on the bagua map.

Orange represents creativity and communication, enthusiasm, and a feeling of warmth and flamboyancy. Combining the powerful energy and stimulation of red with the happiness of yellow, orange as a color is an unsung hero. It is a restorative color. It is optimistic and courageous. It makes you want to take charge and take action. Enveloping your space in orange speaks to your adventurous, outgoing nature. Like red, orange is said to stimulate the appetite, so beware. It is a great color for groups gathering in any type of social setting: dining rooms, kitchens, common areas. Orange represents the fame and reputation quadrant on the bagua map.

Pink revolves around femininity, playfulness, vulnerability, immaturity, and unconditional love. Surrounding yourself with pink speaks of romance and tenderness. It is a good color for a bedroom, or anywhere you need a shot of feminine power. It is a very non-threatening color. You may want to use it when you feel the need to support yourself. Pink represents the marriage and relationship quadrant on the bagua map.

Purple is the regal color. It conjures feelings of power, nobility, luxury, wisdom, transformation, and spirituality, but it can also cause feelings of frustration. With the combination of the tranquility of blue and the energy of red, purple has a magical, mystical quality. It is the perfect color to use if you need to feel emotional security, like a warm blanket, or consider yourself a creative type. Soft shades of purple are healing. Purple also represents wealth and abundance on the bagua map.

Blue's color meaning ties closely to the tranquility of the sea and sky. Stability, safety, unity, harmony, peace, calm, and trustworthiness are communicated by blue. It's a perfect color for a bedroom or anywhere you want to be comforted and calmed. It is the most universally popular color liked by men and women equally.[102]

But blue also evokes depression and can bring about a sense of coldness. This color is an appetite suppressant, so maybe this is the color my kitchen should be! Blue represents knowledge and harmony on the bagua map.

Green is connected to nature, health, and money. Growth, fertility, wellness, stability, rebirth, and generosity are some of the positive color meanings. Green spaces bring balance and "aliveness." The more yellow-hued greens evoke more energetic feelings; think lime and chartreuse. Green is a great color choice for an office. You are able to spend long hours enveloped in green, hopefully concentrating. But negative associations such as jealousy, envy, misfortune, and conceit are also tied to green. Green represents family and new beginnings on the bagua map.

Yellow evokes feelings of happiness, positivity, optimism, and high energy but also of deceit, cowardice, and warning. Bright yellow is certainly attention-getting. It's for risk-takers and someone who loves "newness." Soft yellow, equally as optimistic, might be better for a laid-back personality. Enveloping yourself in yellow emphasizes your desire for individuality. Yellow is representative of health on the bagua map.

Brown is naturally grounding. Color psychology highlights that the color meaning for brown relates to comfort, contentment, resilience, security, and a down-to-earth nature. Dark brown works well in living rooms and family rooms. Earth tones stimulate and promote conversation. Beware: browns can be considered mature and dull, but I disagree. Brown—earth tones—are representative of health on the bagua map.

Black signifies luxury, power, and elegance. It is described as sexy and formal. Those who immerse themselves in black are mysterious, ambiguous, and sophisticated. Be careful. Too much black is too dark (not in a good way) as in death, fear, and a feeling of ominousness. Black is representative of the career and life path on the bagua map.

White exudes purity and cleanliness, modernity, innocence, goodness, and youthfulness. It represents new beginnings and breeds positivity. It is effortless and is often chosen for just that. If you prefer white, you most likely prefer a modern interior. Warmer whites feel cozier, while cooler whites lean toward more formality. White looks right in bathrooms and places you wish to convey cleanliness. It can also be construed as sterile and cold. White is representative of children and creativity on the bagua map.

Gray represents neutrality and balance. It's the color of conformity. It is still clean and neutral, most likely because it falls between black and white without being either. Shades of gray connote intelligence and discipline. Light gray is indecisive, but as the shade gets darker, its personality perks up. It is strong and steady. Gray can be as smoldering and masculine as it can be monotonous and depleting. It plays off other colors well for an inviting environment. Gray is representative of travel and helpful people on the bagua map.

Silver evokes fluidity, prestige, wealth, and sensitivity. It is calming but strong. It is reflective but denotes forward-thinking. It represents a sense of style, dignity, and self-refinement. Silver works well with other colors as it reflects back the energy of that which is around it and denotes an ornateness—as do metallics in general. It is similar to gray but more optimistic and lighthearted. Also, like gray, it can be non-committal and bordering on coldness. Silver does not fall on the bagua map.

Gold is a shade signifying achievement. Gold stars and gold metals, gold bars and gold jewelry, gold is the epitome of opulence and success. It is as connected to high self-worth as it is to having integrity, a sense of right and wrong, honoring tradition, and being part of family tradition. Gold exudes self-confidence. It also does not fall on the bagua map.[103]

If you are interested in the idea of using color to create an emotionally healthy home, choose a predominant color based on your attraction to that color, how that color makes you feel, and the primary function of the room. We know that a bedroom's primary function is to create a sense of calm and enhance slumber. We would not put energizing colors in there, like bright reds or yellows (as our predominant color). We know we feel more relaxed, enveloped in blues and greens or the soft tones of warm colors and neutrals.

Secondary colors used in smaller amounts can be anything your heart desires. Maybe you have a sense of playfulness that you want to explore. Pattern or bright colors are not exempt from the bedroom, but I do suggest using them gingerly to maintain the sense of calm you are creating unless, of course, you have a "go bold or go home" personality, and the stimulation is what gets you out of bed in the morning. There are no hard and fast rules. Stay true to your authenticity.

We now know unequivocally that everything is energy and everything is interconnected. Color and basic design principles are additional tools in your ever-growing toolbox, there to empower you, enrich your life and steer you on your journey toward aligning happiness and authenticity in your home.

TAKEAWAYS

- Color is a nonverbal language unto itself.

- Color has the power to change our moods and enhance our well-being.

- If you are primarily using neutrals, play with texture.

- Light has an impact on the depth of color variation. View color samples in all different kinds of light around the room.

- What color are you most comfortable surrounded by?

- Color doesn't stop at the top of your wall. The ceiling (the fifth wall) is another place to think about color.

12

STAY CALM AND THINK GREEN

The greatest danger to our future is apathy.
—Jane Goodall

GREEN IS ASSOCIATED WITH HEALTH AND WELL-BEing, including all things good for the planet. It is no surprise that we use the word green when describing being conscious of the products we consume, the building materials we use, the lowering of toxins in and around us, and the mindfulness that everything we do affects everyone and everything. Going green, being green… stay calm and think green.

Have you ever been sad or upset and discovered that a walk in nature helped shift your mood? It's a natural antidepressant. Having the visual cues of nature around you has a soothing effect. According to Dr. Jason Strauss, "Having something pleasant to focus on like trees and greenery helps distract your mind from negative thinking, so your thoughts become less filled with worry."[104]

When you are forced to slow down, you are simplifying what your mind complicates. Sometimes simplicity is anything but simple. Being in nature helps us listen to our intuition. It is another way to find stillness and go within. In the stillness, we are able to hear our inner intelligence. Stillness speaks volumes. Inviting stillness into our day is like inviting the sun to shine on what our higher self is planting. Spending time outside, in nature, or seeking out greenspace, improves physical, mental, and spiritual well-being. Nature was Frank Lloyd Wright's main source of inspiration; it permeated everything he designed. Considered the father of organic architecture, Frank Lloyd Wright, understood that when he said, *"Nature is my manifestation of God. I go to nature every day for inspiration in the day's work."*[105]

Modernist architect Richard Neutra understood that our psyche and our health are directly affected by our interiors. He suggested that design "seems to be the way into trouble, and it may be the way out."[106] He was a pioneer of environmental psychology, emphasizing the importance of the connectivity of our environments to our overall health. Wright and Neutra share architectural philosophies deeply connected to nature. We continue to be positively influenced by their philosophy generations later.

While Wright was "seamlessly connecting architecture and the environment," Neutra believed he was able to destabilize the barriers between the psyche and its natural surroundings in such a way that psychic energy would be allowed to float freely."[107] They were the early adopters of what is now called environmental psychology; its meaning is derived from the interplay between people and their environments.

Nature provides a soothing experience. Architecture designed for your well-being and overall holistic health acknowledges that our exposure to trees, fresh air, green space, mountains, and bodies of water—whether real or replicated—reminds us of this. Studies back up the fact that viewing natural environments speeds up the body's ability to heal, is good for our immune system, and reduces stress, anxiety, and fatigue.[108]

Biophilia, or man's experience in nature, is central to a holistically healthy environment. We naturally want to seek connections to nature. If you love a live-edge table that incorporates a section of an actual tree, a vertical herb garden, or an end table made of stone— then you are a lover of biophilic design. We spend so much time indoors, in front of computer screens, in cars, alone, that we need to make an effort to reconnect to nature. This includes not only natural things but all living things. After all, biophilia means love of life and the living world. It is foundational to the human spirit to live with natural materials, the patterns and shapes found in nature, and representations of life that touch the senses.[109]

Among the advantages of incorporating biophilia into your living or working space are these sorts of health benefits. If food is medicine, design is medicine too. We want always to be in the process of healing, doing what we know is good for our bodies because we understand that directly correlates to what is good for our souls.

You need to consider such things as whether the soil your food was grown in has been sprayed with pesticides and herbicides as well as whether there are chemicals in the water we drink and pollution in the air we breathe. This constant toxic onslaught has a price, and we are paying it dearly. These toxins are inflammatory and damaging to the endocrine system. They also wreak havoc on hormones and affect the reproductive system. Geneticists are looking to inflammation, viruses, and even air pollution as possible factors in the uptick of disease.[110] All kinds of autoimmune diseases are soaring. Cancer and Alzheimer's have been linked to our near-constant toxin exposure. Scientists believe that some man-made environmental compounds can be associated directly or indirectly with Alzheimer's disease, including various insecticides, industrial and commercial pollutants, antimicrobials, heavy metals, and air pollutants.[111]

These chemicals persist in the environment long after initial use, causing toxicity to flora and fauna. Our soil has been raped of most of its nutrients. I certainly believe the causes of these illnesses are a combination of many factors: genetic, lifestyle, and environmental. University of California researcher Dr. Judith Stern said: "*Genetics load the gun but environment pulls the trigger.*"[112]

Our genetic predisposition to illness, in combination with our choices and actions, determine why some of us get sick, and others do not, as well as why each of us can be exposed to the same thing, but our response can be markedly different.

As I became more educated, I learned to ask a lot of questions and always do my research when purchasing something for my home or for a client. Years ago, I decorated a historic office space and brought in the most beautiful metallic wallpaper to paper a ceiling. It mimicked an antique tin ceiling and gave the office the perfect nod to its pre-war roots. The only problem was the paper's adhesive was so full of chemicals that were unleashed upon application that no one could enter the office due to the overwhelming fumes. My client was working from the conference room, and everyone on that floor suffered from a headache until the smell dissipated—which took about a week with all the windows open and a fan blowing. I just knew we were harming our bodies, breathing the fumes that paper emitted. When you know better, you do better, so I am very conscious now of what goes in the things I purchase.

Volatile organic compounds (VOCs) are very common. I am sure that was what was in the wallpaper. According to the Environmental Protection Agency (EPA), VOCs are emitted as gases from certain solids or liquids. In fact, they may be emitted by a wide array of products, including paints and lacquers, paint strippers, cleaning supplies, household products such as varnishes and wax, mattresses, clothing, cleaning and disinfecting products, building materials (plywood and particleboard), and furnishings, glues, and adhesives.[113]

Soon after my experience with the wallpaper, I discovered the Environmental Working Group and Ecocert. Its mission is to empower people to live healthier lives in a healthier environment. These are good resources to check any time you want to see the ingredients in something you are using. They allow you to search by product, ingredient, or brand, making it very simple. These resources go a long way toward educating consumers.

We can be ignorant no longer because our health is at risk. It is important that we force these agencies to act promptly to reduce exposure to toxic chemicals linked to cancer, hormonal disruptions, respiratory disease, birth defects, and other health issues.[114]

When we stand up and use our voices and our dollars against company practices that have the potential to hurt us, we can make a change.

Clean, non-toxic, certified organic, biodegradable, non-GMO (genetically modified organism), eco-friendly, eco-conscious, environmentally friendly, renewable, responsibly sourced, sustainable, sustainably harvested—are all words we want to look for if we are trying to be informed consumers. But many packaging terms aren't FDA regulated, and companies often market their products dishonestly. This is a huge problem. In the US, this is allowed, whereas other countries have banned this deceptive practice. Why is America lagging behind?

The misuse of terms like these are a ploy to get the consumer to believe something without scientific proof.

Other generic terms such as: all natural, good for you, organic, healthy, humanely raised, heart healthy, farm raised, free range, and fair trade can cause your head to explode! Read labels, do your research and do the best you can. An educated consumer is the best consumer. We read these labels and assume the products we purchase are tested for safety before they land on store shelves. We are not being told the truth. I hope I have convinced you that a shocking number of dangerous chemicals hide in everything from home improvement items to cosmetics, personal care products, and household items.

Our bodies are crying out for help. I know I am painting a dark picture, but we have to think about the future: the world we are leaving to our children and grandchildren. All is not lost. What can we do?

We can think green and act now. Going green refers to cleaning up our use of everyday items that, over time, lead to an overload of toxins that stress our bodies and stress our planet.

Ask questions of manufacturers about products you bring into your home. Little by little, one step by one step, you will begin to understand what changes you can make. I have adopted a 70/30 rule for myself. We don't live in a bubble. I am still going to get my hair colored, but I got rid of a chemical-laden mattress.

It is not uncommon for items such as wallpaper, paint, and building materials in your home to be made with flame retardants, formaldehydes, parabens, and other chemicals. Some chemicals in this classification are ingredients in vinyl, wood varnishes, lacquers, and air fresheners as well. Imagine plugging a popular air freshener into a wall outlet and thinking you are freshening the scent in the air, when in fact, you are placing more chemicals into the air and then breathing them. Look for these types of products made with essential oils instead.

Building a home or furnishing one can feel like a daunting task in and of itself. Before you even begin selecting items, you must give thought to how these things are made, where they're made, and what they are made from. These products could be giving off gases that your family, your guests, and pets will absorb into their bodies. They're bad for you, and they're bad for the environment.

As global warming and climate change continue to rise at an alarming rate, the idea of sustainability has also become an immediate priority. For this reason, many manufacturers committed to sustainability practices for a cleaner, greener Earth have committed to minimizing carbon emissions and reducing pollutants and have removed harmful chemicals from their goods.

"Better building equals better lives" is the mission statement of the US Green Building Council. Remember this mantra.[115]

When it comes to sustainable interior design, you can plan efficient use of space and choose materials with low environmental impact that reduces energy consumption and pollution. The interior design industry is shifting, and there are so many more options in fashion-forward home goods that are sustainable, beautiful, and made to last whether you adhere to a less is more minimalist aesthetic, or a more is more maximalist aesthetic.

As an interior designer, I am committed to this for my clients; as a consumer, I am committed to this for myself and my family. It is really quite simple: let in the good, keep out the bad. I would also argue that "buying the best you can afford" or maybe pushing the budget a little further than you are comfortable with is also a sustainable process to avoid adding more poorly made items to a land-fill. Well-made furniture lasts a lifetime! Incorporating antiques not only helps to create a unique space but is green too. Classic pieces of furniture can be handed down from generation to generation, never going out of style. Stay away from trends for big-ticket items and buy what you love. Quality over quantity is a lesson worth learning.

Healthy Inside and Out

We spend almost 90 percent of our time indoors. Shouldn't we spend that time in as healthy and lovely an environment as possible? Shouldn't that environment not only be good for our health but be good for our souls? To be at home and in nature may be the path to Nirvana.

But what can you do to incorporate healthier, greener options into your everyday environment? If you're going to do just one thing immediately, make the switch to more energy-efficient light bulbs. Compact fluorescent light bulbs are energy efficient, but they're awful! Incandescent bulbs are being phased out for not being energy efficient enough. LED bulbs and halogens are good alternatives. I love them for their bright white light. Although these bulbs cost more upfront than incandescent bulbs, they also last about 10 times longer. Each has pros and cons, so know what your needs are and control these lights with a dimmer as much as you can.

Below is an extensive list of some of the things you might want to consider doing to lessen your toxic load. Do not get overwhelmed and feel like you must do all of these things. As with everything I talk about in this book, choose what resonates with you, begin there and see where it leads you.

What are you willing to do? What are you not willing to do? What works with your lifestyle or excites you rather than feeling like it is too much of a chore?

- Clean and vacuum rugs regularly. Make sure your vacuum has strong suction and a HEPA filter. Natural floors are best.

- Proper insulation keeps home costs down. Do you know what kind or how much insulation you have?

- Choose low or no VOC paints and sustainable products for all your renovation needs.

- Add air purifiers for clean air; fresh is best!

- Organic mattresses and bedding are a wise investment considering we spend nearly one-third of our life in bed.

- When was the last time you had your air ducts cleaned or tested for radon? This colorless, odorless gas comes from the natural breakdown of the soil and rock underneath your home. Any home can have a radon gas problem. A simple at-home test kit will do the job.

- Toss the Teflon, switch to other cookware now: stainless steel, anodized aluminum, copper-coated pans, cast iron, or enamel-coated iron. The nonstick coating causes problems.

- Water filters can protect you from impurities in your water, but there is some debate as to whether they purify the pollutants in your area that specifically affect you. An at-home water sample test will help identify what you actually need to remove from the water, then choose a water filtration system accordingly.

- Choose organic! We always want to choose organic foods but don't forget things like lawn sprays, dry cleaners, and mattresses.

- Are your appliances Energy Star certified? Improving the energy efficiency of your home most certainly will save you money, and Uncle Sam may reward you in the form of tax credits.

- Kill the energy vampires: the electronics that are plugged in when not in use. Unplug what you can. Our cellphones, microwaves, older televisions, Wi-Fi routers, computers, and other appliances send out low-level radiation. Many people experience electric-and-magnetic-field (EMF) sensitivity that may manifest as anything from headaches to heart arrhythmia.[116]

- Regulate your air conditioning and heat on a programmable timer, so you are not running it during times when you are not in your home or asleep. Use drapes and curtains to achieve a similar effect.

- Plug up pesky air leaks. Preventing cooled and warm air from escaping your home helps keep your HVAC system from having to constantly work to maintain a desirable indoor temperature.

- Natural materials are always a better choice over synthetic materials. Think cotton, wool, bamboo, leather, silk, hemp, linen, jute, mohair, cashmere. Natural fibers are environmentally sustainable. The majority of natural fabrics are biodegradable, moisture-wicking, breathable, durable, heat-responsive, and naturally repellent to mold and dirt. Some are naturally hypoallergenic, making them good choices for those with allergies or illnesses.

- Be vigilant so that there is NO mold in your home or workplace at all, ever!

- Read labels to choose the least toxic things you can. It helps to be able to understand what the ingredients are in your products. Can you read and understand the ingredients? Can you eat them?

- Look for "green" cleaning products that do not contain chlorine or ammonia. Choose ones that say "petroleum-free," "biodegradable," or "phosphate-free." Consider making your own cleaning solutions. Just mix a few tablespoons of white distilled vinegar with warm water and a few drops of your favorite essential oil.

- Consider solar panels. Solar power can be harnessed to create electricity for your home to heat water and to improve indoor lighting, all while saving you money in the long run.

- Compost anyone? Cut your carbon footprint by composting food scraps (except meat) in a backyard composting bin or even a worm bin.

- Buying antiques is green. Anything previously owned cuts down on waste.

- Ditch the air fresheners and candles whose fragrances do not come from natural ingredients like essential oils.

- Fix anything leaking. Don't allow money to go down the drain along with the water.

- Reduce, reuse, and recycle.

- Reduce your use of all plastic. Bisphenol A (BPA) lurks in plastic food storage containers, the lining of cans, toys, packaging, and so much more. Do not—I repeat—do not microwave food in plastic containers. The heat may force chemicals to leach into your food. Nobody wants that.

Happiness Can Be Found in a Plant

Plants radiate harmonious energy simply by being living things. According to feng shui principles, they help welcome in new opportunities, ground your space, and reduce stress. If you've ever wondered why plant-filled spaces bring you joy, this might have something to do with it. Plants literally "liven" up any space they occupy.

Did you know that many house plants can improve the quality of your air by increasing oxygen levels? Some plants are even more powerful than others at removing toxic chemicals like benzene, formaldehyde, and ammonia from the air, according to a NASA study. In a six-month study of a plant-filled room compared with a room without plants, the levels of airborne microbes and bacteria were 50 percent higher in the room without plants. Plants in the home also increase humidity, which reduces irritation from dry sinuses, reduces the severity of asthma, and reduces congestion."[117]

Occupants of rooms with plants recover faster from illness, and studies have shown that plants promote a higher level of focus. They are the best-looking air filter! They sit beautifully and silently, working their magic, removing pollutants in the air and helping to create a sense of calm.

Some popular plants to consider from a wellness and feng shui perspective are:

Air Plan: A perfect combination of wind and water. All these plants need is a little spritz of H2O to remain healthy.

Aloe Vera: We know it's good for our skin, but this plant is also super purifying in your home. The aloe is a succulent, and it combats bad luck and negative energy.

Bamboo plant: Lucky bamboo is probably the most closely related to feng shui principles. It's easy to care for, and you can train it into shapes. Lucky bamboo is believed to bring harmony among the five feng shui elements of water, fire, earth, wood, and metal for a more positive life experience. Place it in the creativity, wealth, or health gua. It was rated No. 1 in NASA's test for removing formaldehyde from the air.[118]

Boston Fern is a powerhouse for purifying all kinds of pollutants, including cigarette smoke. The compounds are absorbed through the plant's leaves.

English Ivy isn't just for the outdoors. Ivy indoors helps to purify the air and absorbs allergens and mold. It thrives in the sun. It was rated No. 1 for removing benzene from the air.[119]

Ficus comes in many different varieties. It makes for a great bonsai. Design aficionados love a fig tree, although these trees can be finicky. Ficus and ginseng are good for luck. And the ficus is great for air quality cleansing.

Golden pothos is easy to care for. Its heart-shaped leaves, reflecting self-love and kindness, are attractive, and the plant itself is quite forgiving if you don't have a green thumb. It is believed that the plant brings luck, happiness, prosperity, and wealth.

Jade is also called the money tree because its round leaves look like coins and are said to summon fortune. It is the most popular plant in feng shui for obvious reasons and is best placed in a wealth corner, no surprise. It produces positive energy with its well-rooted and vibrant new growth.

Mass cane or **corn plant** is the easiest plant to grow, which makes it the most popular to own.

Orange Tree: Citrus in general, symbolizes abundance and luck. It should be placed in your health or wealth gua, indoors or out.

Orchids are amazing anywhere. They are symbols of creativity, fertility, and good fortune. Based on the color of the petals you choose, place them where you want the attraction indicated by their petals to occur: pink (two stems) for love, yellow for health, purple for wealth. Double the pleasure, double the energy.

Peace lily: The name invites peace and positive vibes, which makes it a good wood element to incorporate. The flower is beautiful. The peace lily invites peace and growth in and encourages toxins out. It's a great purifier.

Rubber plant is a member of the fig family. It is a superb low-maintenance plant that supports healing and growth.

Snake plant conjures memories of my grandparents to me, but for most, it's sword-like leaves emote the feeling of protection. This plant is a good option to position by your electronics as it releases negative ions. The snake plant releases oxygen at night, so this is a perfect purifier plant for bedrooms, though feng shui says steer clear of plants in a bedroom.

Spider plant represents abundance and giving. Its off-shoots are able to sprout easily. According to feng shui it is good for calling in wealth and prosperity. The spider plant is one of the top varieties for removing VOCs and other pollutants from indoor air.[120]

Magic happens in the garden. Your yard should be a place of pleasure and feng shui principles. It should be neat, free of extraneous stuff, beautiful to your eye, and a place of peace. Design your yard or outdoor space to be a place for play and socializing, rest and relaxation. Everything that applies inside your home applies to your outdoors as well. It is not a separate space but part of the whole. Gardening helps heal depression, grief, and anxiety, and it improves physical and mental health.[121] I like to think of it as a heart-smart, low-impact activity.

As a matter of fact, the garden is a beautiful metaphor for life. According to British plantswoman Beth Chatto, creator of exquisite gardens in Essex, England, and originator of the saying, "Right plant, right place,"[122] "We are like plants. We need varying degrees of the right conditions: light, air quality, water, sun or shade, and space in which to grow and flourish."

If all the elements are in our favor, we will thrive. If not, we wither. If you are a sun lover who is used to being close to water, you would most likely be unhappy feeling landlocked in the middle of the country. If you are an avid hiker who loves peaks and valleys, you will not fare well in an area where the topography is flat. We humans thrive in different conditions. We should know what those conditions are.

The Benefits of a Garden

I distinctly remember how devastated I felt when my parents told me they were getting a divorce. It didn't matter that I was an adult at that point. I felt what a child feels. I was heartbroken. I created an elaborate garden in the corner of my backyard that year. It became my refuge. As I cried and dug in, I let go of any expectations I had about my family moving forward as I had always assumed. My life was about to change, and there was nothing I could do about it. The physical act of creating the garden was my "soul purpose" for those few months. As I was creating, I was healing.

I heard many a story of gardens flourishing around the country as the pandemic took hold. Many found comfort and beauty in sowing seeds in the garden. Seeing blossoms appear or harvesting food to sustain families brings with it a certain pride and joy; there really is a satisfying feeling of accomplishment. If we reap what we sow, we best choose that which nourishes us.

Sustainable Living Is Here to Stay

Gardens are a distinct part of sustainable living. They allow you to spend time in the outdoors, appreciating nature and growing your own flowers, plants, and even food.

Gardens lead you to consider how you can do your part to consume less, create less waste, and reduce your environmental impact. Our symbiotic relationship with our Earth is a delicate one. Mother Earth needs us now more than ever.

Small steps can make a big impact. Being mindful of how and what you consume is also a big part of sustainability. This is summed up as "Recycling, reducing, and reusing waste will help save money, energy and natural resources," according to the US Environmental Protection Agency.[123]

It isn't enough to simply change the products you use. Living greener is going to require a new way of thinking, a paradigm shift. The old way doesn't work, and a new normal must stand in its place. We must heed the warning that the planet is giving us. Let's act out less and listen more.

When, briefly, people became still, forced indoors, at the start of the COVID-19 pandemic, the Earth miraculously began to recover: the sky became bluer, oceans became clearer, animals flourished. We began to recover because we are one with the earth.

We must change the way we view the world and our part in it, especially as a consumer. Look at the bigger picture. We can all practice Earth stewardship by thinking globally of the large-scale effects on the environment, acting locally in terms of purchases, and understanding that what's good for the planet is good for us, too.

TAKEAWAYS

- Plants are activating energy, so use them whenever you want to "lift" the energy of an area. For this reason, in feng shui, plants in bedrooms are frowned upon. You want calming energy in the bedroom.

- Reduce your toxic load now; begin slowly if it feels overwhelming.

- Always be thinking green and making sustainability a priority. It is good for you. It is good for the planet.

- Make your health a priority!

- Educate yourself on which chemicals are going into your body, which may be going into your home.

- Viewing nature, real or replicated, speeds up the body's ability to heal and has a plethora of restorative benefits.

- Certain plants help improve air quality, remove chemicals, and are good feng shui.

- Incorporate biophilic design, which essentially means staying close to nature.

13

BEING IN FLOW

Remember, the entrance door to the sanctuary is inside you.
—Attributed to Rumi

WHAT WE SPEAK ABOUT WITHIN OUR HOMES LIN-
gers long after the conversations have ended. What we nourish ourselves
with—body, mind, and soul—impacts us in myriad ways. What we
think about ourselves and others has implications reaching further than
our minds. We put that energy out into the universe. Simply making a
conscious effort to shift the conversation from negative and depleting
to positive and enhancing can make a difference in the energy coming
from both you and your home. The result of that will be living from a
state of flow. It's a highly enjoyable state of being. Once you feel flow,
you never want to go back.

In flow, you are engaged in life. Mihaly Csikszentmihalyi, the father
of the concept of the flow state, likens it to other Zen states of mind
known to the Buddhist, Taoist, and the Hindu. It is "the holistic

sensation that people feel when they act with total involvement."[124]

Finding flow allows you to feel like you are stretching yourself. What this means is that the state or activity you are engaged in is difficult but not too difficult. Challenging yourself, pushing, pursuing personal growth, and continuing to learn new skills: these should be lifelong pursuits. I love this on so many levels. Your feeling state will reflect this by giving you positive feedback.

The belief is that if you are too challenged, you'll give up in frustration. If you are not challenged enough, you'll give up from boredom. But, if you are challenged just the right amount, you will find balance, feel deep satisfaction, and find ways to replicate the experience.

This state allows you immediate feedback, good or bad. If the sensation is bad, you can course-correct immediately to find the more pleasurable state. We should be seeking this at all times, in an effort to live in flow.

Because your home makes you feel a certain way just by being present there, when you are in flow, your home is in flow. You cannot be in flow within your home if your feeling state is not registering a high positive for you. Seeking pleasure is a by-product of really going within and doing the hard—possibly uncomfortable—work of getting to know yourself on a deeper level. I am not at all speaking of a hedonist who is seeking pleasure for pleasure's sake and immediate gratification. This kind of gratification is really self-fulfilling and sustainable.

We are willing our reality into existence. We often see things and ourselves through a very narrow lens. Our perception may be limited, information fragmented. When we widen the lens, we are able to observe a fuller, more accurate picture. We filter our reality around our value system, set goals, and take action that is in alignment with those values; we are moving toward our wholeness. We are living our purpose because we are choosing to live by our values. Keeping our mind/body compass in mind, we filter out what we loathe and filter in what we love.

You can look forward to arising each day and enthusiastically observing the beauty of your life story as it unfolds. Moving forward toward goals keeps your vibrational energy high. Performing actionable steps increases the odds that you will attain what you set your mind to. Imagine the outcome, and acting "as if" while you "remain unattached" allows for the law of attraction to play a supporting role on your road to finding your flow.

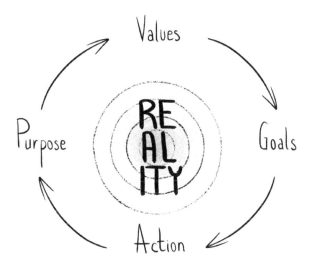

Being in flow, finding your om, and living in authenticity is all about creating a holistic lifestyle in which you are flourishing. Your reality is formed by values, and the goals you set are based on those values. Then, by taking actionable steps, even little ones, that offer fulfillment, you are creating the feeling of purpose. Value-rooted purpose creates fulfillment. That fulfillment equals joy and emotional well-being.

My Home Is in Flow

"I love my home! I never want to leave it, and when I do, I can't wait to return," Sheryl exclaims enthusiastically. I am immediately envious because it is no secret: I wish I felt that way about my own home. I was fascinated by this declaration and wanted to know everything about Sheryl in order to identify how her feelings about her home empowered her so much.

A piece of property became available across the street from the home she raised her family in. When it did, Sheryl and her husband jumped at the chance to build from the ground up, in a neighborhood they already felt attached to. They quickly began designing their forever-home, first on a napkin and then more formally with an architect. They considered every aspect of what would make them happy, what best expressed them as individuals and as a couple.

Today, Jim has a man cave, Sheryl a she-shed. There are areas in their home conducive for alone time and places to come together as a couple and with extended family and friends. They took into consideration ideas about aging in place and having a place for their grandchildren. They considered everything that they knew would make them happy at home.

Inside the light-filled, traditional colonial, Sheryl, who took nothing with her when she moved across the street, filled her new living space only with things that gave her joy or were useful and necessary. Photos of family and friends reminded her daily of the love she feels surrounded by, and new kitchen appliances fueled the creative cooking hobby she adopted once she became an empty nester. Now she had the luxury of making each space as joy-filled as possible without kids' possessions cluttering everything. She was free to see what gave her pleasure. She knew herself really well but was always curious to see if there was more to discover. It is no coincidence that she uncovered a love of entertaining she had not experienced in her former, smaller home.

Sheryl and Jim had lots of friends nearby and felt tied to their tight-knit community. You can achieve a longer and more fulfilling life—among other benefits—when you are happy, fulfilled, have community support and, on top of that, a living space you love.

This experience with building their dream home became an exploratory exercise in what filled Sheryl. She listened to her intuition and went with it. She replaced expectation with appreciation.

That kind of appreciation can also be referred to as gratitude. You don't have to wait to build your dream home to do this, and it should be a daily practice. Sheryl will tell you that she feels fulfilled because she creates that fulfillment for herself. She has a strong mind/body connection and the awareness to go within. Her intuition is so fine-tuned that every decision is made based on an awareness to pursue self-satisfaction.

"I make happiness for myself," Sheryl said when pressed for more information during a conversation. "Not that everything is perfect. Nothing and no one is perfect, but I trust my judgment."

I think, ultimately, what defines your ability to be happy and fulfilled is having and incorporating simple tools into your life, in a realistic way, every day. Sheryl is happy enough. Things are good enough. She has a career that fulfills her and gives her pleasure. She accepts what is and surrenders to what isn't. She sets her sights on what she knows she can attain—and attains it—therefore, she is rarely disappointed. Some would call that major manifestation power at work! What Sheryl doesn't do is sweat the small stuff. She doesn't indulge in thinking thoughts that do not serve her higher needs. She is a realist and is pragmatic. She knows with every fiber of her being that when she sets a goal, she is damn well going to get it.

In Chapter 5, I mentioned going to a party where a psychic told me of my future. I think Sheryl may have been at that same party. Maybe the psychic would give her the exact same reading she gave me: "You will have everything you need." And maybe Sheryl, without question, would have believed her. Maybe Sheryl has everything she needs because she has made up her mind there is no other option. Sheryl's was wholly fulfilled because her experiences met or exceeded her expectations.

When you surrender to what is, ease fills the places that worry and "what ifs" and "why me" used to fill. The joy of surrender means the ability to let go: you find exactly what you need—or it finds you.

Finding Your Flow

Living authentically is the belief that you are doing the best you can with what you have been given. Every day brings a new opportunity to choose what feels best, to be the best version of yourself. If that doesn't happen, there's always the following day. Happiness comes and goes; sadness comes and goes. Meet yourself wherever you are. Finding the balance and accepting what you cannot change will never steer you wrong as you seek out your North Star.

I instilled in myself a growth mindset. By not taking no for an answer, by not taking what doctors told me at face value, by not settling for less than what I believe I deserved, I baby-stepped my way to better health and happiness. I managed to manifest a life that makes me so much happier, so much more fulfilled, so much more grateful. I willed it into existence, and you can, too.

There is an anonymous quote that is often misattributed to Abraham Lincoln that says, "*I am not bound to succeed, but I am bound to live up to what light I have.*"[125]

Maybe what you really want is to feel that you are doing the best you can, not necessarily to succeed, just to feel worthy. And ironically, when you do that, you are actually more likely to succeed. Success means different things to different people. Whatever your definition is for you, there is absolutely no way you can't reach it when you put all these elements into practice.

Be mindful that the fluidity of life will take you where you need to go. Happy in the high moments, rightfully sad in the unhappy moments, but always moving through space, day-by-day, toward your North Star with the knowledge that the little ordinary events are cumulatively leading you to where you were meant to be.

By understanding the interconnection of all the elements I have laid out, and moving through them step-by-step, making sure my mind, body, spirit, and space were all aligned, I managed to manifest not a new home but a more fulfilling lifestyle, which ultimately is what I really wanted after all. By staying in the house and taking the power out of my thoughts surrounding my "stuckness," I realized that the house is manageable financially and allows me the ability to do other things. By staying in my home, I am able to travel, visit my children and friends, rent a little place in Florida for the winter. These are the things that really enrich my life. This is what was meant for me, though I may not have seen it at first. Somebody could have told me this, and I wouldn't have owned it because I didn't feel it. I had to do the work on myself. From my pain, physically and emotionally, I resolved to learn how to be the best version of me.

From each experience and the knowledge I gained from it, I finally understood I was not living in alignment with one of my most important values. I value new experiences, the excitement of discovery. When I was working from home and not connecting with others enough, my curiosity and fulfillment wanned. Not living in alignment with my core values made me unfulfilled, and in this "in-between" state, I projected my dissatisfaction onto my home. I blamed the house and did not see my part in the state of my unrest.

Some may be lucky enough to have been given the necessary mindful tools as a child. Those tools become a part of us, like a cloak we wear, like Joseph's Technicolor dream coat. Like a rainbow, we slip in and out of the sun and clouds. We are self-confident, self-aware, and able to pivot when life takes its inevitable twists and turns.

But some may need more help. Maybe you were not given the tools you require by your parents or mentors. You were not inclined to believe in your own magnificence and worth because it was not part of your lexicon growing up. This language of acknowledgment did not envelope you in the warmth of unconditional love and acceptance. But you can give it to yourself. Everything we need is within!

We can be the biggest saboteur to our own success, but we don't need to be.

According to Dr. Joe Dispenza, "Thoughts are the language of the brain, feelings are the language of the body." As the creator of your more "self-aware" life, your healthier thinking and feeling is changing the outcome of your reality. Each time you make a choice that is in alignment with your vision of your future idea of yourself, you are rewiring your brain to think, act, and feel like that person you're actually becoming. When you consciously live from a new space, you not only see yourself from a fresh perspective, but you'll also intentionally create behaviors that are in alignment with your new identity.

To create spaciousness in your life and in your home, you must live from a place of clarity and authenticity. You are infinite possibility. Be present. Come home to breath, mindfulness, intention, gratitude—and watch the world change within and around you.

Consider this your fork in the road. Mindfulness allows you to take a step back. It is powerful to know what you are feeling when you feel it, recognize your thoughts when you begin thinking them. Then, you can choose to strengthen ways that empower you, let go of that that does not serve to empower you, and find the wisdom to know the difference.

Anything that makes you feel *less than* is an illusion. Run to joy, run to happiness, run to good health, run to people who love you for you, through the good times and the bad. Feather your nest in a way that brings you peace and deep satisfaction.

It is never too late to just begin. You can learn these things and put them into practice at any time. Begin anywhere because you have learned that since all these elements are connected, one step forward will lead you to the next, then the next. Changing behavior to reach your goals happens incrementally. Keep your eye on the prize, be intentional, and trust it will happen.

Putting this into practice, I now think of my home as a place of respite until the next adventure, and that suits me just fine. I absolutely believe inner work lends itself to the ability to connect externally. When your home environment inspires you to live in a way that supports your dreams and aspirations, then you manifest and move in the direction of your more actualized self.

As I've said before, your home should be your point of view, your narrative, and an expression of your authenticity. It should be a narrative about how you see the world around you that you want to share.

Think of it as an exclamation mark on your life being well-lived.

I'm telling you this, in case you need to hear it: You are the bold creator of your beautiful life. You are a powerful, wise, loving, creative, compassionate, intelligent spirit!

I have no doubt that whatever you may be struggling with, there are signs pointing you to your North Star. You are on a hero's journey. You have to want to be open-minded enough to see the signs, feel the signs, follow your intuition, your curiosity, your heart. Step-by-step, you move through the world looking for the answers you seek, going boldly into the future when you happen upon an "aha moment." That's when you realize you did the work that took you right where you were meant to be. Before this moment becomes a memory—dig in.

I read this anonymous quote in a newsletter once, and it just resonated with me:

> *"One day, you wake up, and you're in this place. You're in this place where everything feels right. Your heart is calm. Your soul is lit. Your thoughts are positive. Your vision is clear. You're at peace, at peace with where you've been, at peace with what you've been through, and at peace with where you're headed."*

And that means you are headed authentically hOMe.

A Final Exercise: Home as Self-Portrait

Ask yourself this: What do I associate with home? What colors? What smells? What brings you joy? What precious memories do you want to embrace? Think about all these things as they pertain to your emotional, physical, and spiritual needs. With this in mind, how would you want to fill your home? This is what I did.

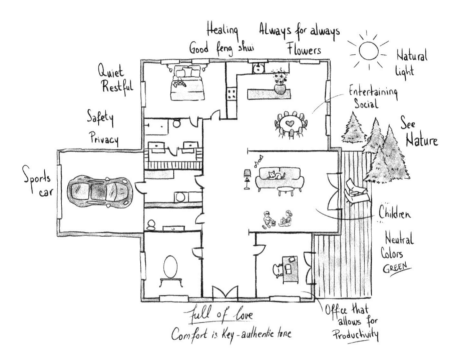

What would your home look like if you were to prioritize what you need and want in order to create an environment that you want to come back to again and again?

Add any elements to the blank floor plan below to create your ideal environment.

My Ideal Home Has:

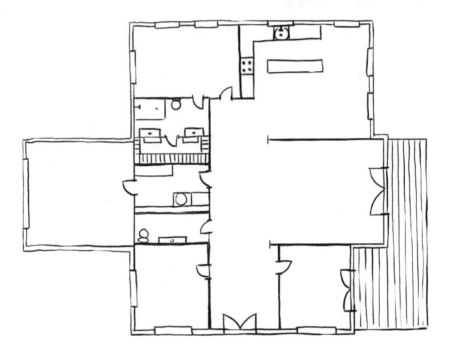

RESOURCES

1   Sahara Rose, *The Highest Self Podcast*, "I Am Sahara Rose," accessed January 25, 2021.

2   *Runaway Bride*, dir. Garry Marshall. Paramount Pictures, 1999.

3   Joshua J. Mark, "Upanishads," Ancient History Encyclopedia (Ancient History Encyclopedia, March 20, 2021), https://www.ancient.eu/Upanishads/.

4   Kripalu Center for Yoga & Health, "The Meaning of 'Om'," HuffPost (HuffPost, January 23, 2014), https://www.huffpost.com/entry/meaning-of-om_b_4177447.

5   Leonard P. Kessler, *Mr. Pine's Purple House* (Cynthiana, KY: Purple House Books, 2014).

6   "Holism," Merriam-Webster (Merriam-Webster), accessed January 31, 2021, https://www.merriam-webster.com/dictionary/holism.

7   Marilia Carabotti, et al., "The gut-brain axis: interactions between enteric microbiota, central and enteric nervous systems," *Annals of Gastroenterology* 28, no. 2, 2015.

8   "What Causes Dysbiosis and How Is It Treated? - Healthline," accessed March 20, 2021, https://www.healthline.com/health/digestive-health/dysbiosis.

9   Amanda MacMillan, "It's Official: Happiness Really Can Improve Health," *Time*, July 20, 2017, https://time.com/4866693/happiness-improves-health/.

10 Bill Edgar, "Biblical Wisdom: Proverbs 24:3-4," Geneva College, June 5, 2019.

11 Lenny R. Vartanian, et al., "Clutter, Chaos, and Overconsumption: The Role of Mind-Set in Stressful and Chaotic Food Environments," *Environments and Behavior* 49, no. 2, 2016.

12   Marie Helwig-Larsen, "Why Denmark dominates the World Happiness Report rankings year after year," *The Conversation,* March 20, 2018.

13   Anna Altman, "The Year of Hygge, The Danish Obsession with Getting Cozy," The *New Yorker,* December 18, 2016.

14   "Self Care – Hygge or The Danish and Norwegian Art of Coziness and Conviviality," *Conscious by Chloé,* November 28, 2018.

15   Altman, "The Year of Hygge."

16   Ingrid K. Williams, "Danish Hygge Is So Last Year. Say Hello to Swedish Mys," The *New York Times,* November 25, 2020.

17   Ursula Hartenberger, "Why buildings matter," The *Guardian,* July 1, 2011.

18   "Environment," *Psychology Today,* accessed January 26, 2021.

19   L. Scannell, et al., "Defining place attachment: A tripartite organizing framework," *Journal of Environmental Psychology* 30, no. 1, 2010.

20   Toby Israel, *Some Place Like Home: Using Design Psychology to Create Ideal Places* (Design Psychology Press, 2010).

21   Amy Croffey, "How to care for jade plants," *Better Home and Gardens,* December 12, 2019.

22   Marie Kondo, *The Life-Changing Magic of Tidying Up: The Japanese Art of Decluttering and Organizing* (Berkeley, CA: Ten Speed Press, 2014).

23   Rachel Pannett and Rhiannon Hoyle, "Marie Kondo Isn't Sparking Joy for Thrift Stores," The *Wall Street Journal,* March 6, 2019.

24   Fugen Neziroglu, "Hoarding: The Basics," Anxiety and Depression Association of America, accessed January 26, 2021.

25   "Hoarding Disorder," Mayo Clinic, accessed January 26, 2021.

26   Irina Gonzalez, "What Is Chi Energy? Everything You Need to Know About the Ancient Chinese Term," *O* Magazine, April 8, 2019.

27   Susan Krauss Whitbourne, "5 Reasons to Clear the Clutter Out of Your Life," *Psychology Today,* May 13, 2017.

28   Mary MacVean, "For many people, gathering possessions is just the stuff of life," *Los Angeles Times,* March 21, 2014.

29   Emilie Le Beau Lucchesi, "The Unbearable Heaviness of Clutter," *New York Times,* January 3, 2019.

30   "Stress management," Mayo Clinic, accessed January 27, 2021.

31   Catherine A. Roster , et al., "The dark side of home: Assessing possession 'clutter' on subjective well-being," *Journal of Environmental Psychology* 46, 2016.

32   Neringa, Antanaityte, "Mind matters: How to Effortlessly Have More Positive Thoughts," TLEX Institute, accessed January 27, 2021.

33   Thubten, Chodron, *Taming the Monkey Mind* (Scotland: Tynron Press, 1995).

34   Ibid.

35   Regina Bailey, "Bacteria: Friend or Foe?" *ThoughtCo,* June 24, 2018.

36 Elizabeth Scott, "What Is the Law of Attraction?" *Very Well Mind*, November 18, 2020.

37 Mike Dooley, *Playing the Matrix: A Program for Living Deliberately and Creating Consciously* (Carlsbad, CA: Hay House, 2017).

38 Andreas Komninos, "Our Three Brains – The Reptilian Brain," Interaction Design, January 6, 2021.

39 Nicole Haloupek, "What is the amygdala?" *Live Science*, January 21, 2020.

40 Seth Godin, *Linchpin: Are You Indispensable?* (New York: Portfolio, 2011).

41 Martha Beck, *Steering by Starlight: The Science and Magic of Finding Your Destiny.* (Emmaus, PA: Rodale Books, 2009).

42 Kent C. Berridge and Morten L. Kringelbach, "Pleasure systems in the brain," *Neuron* 86, no. 3, 2015.

43 Huan Song, et al., "Association of Stress-Related Disorders With Subsequent Autoimmune Disease," *JAMA* 319, no. 23, 2018.

44 "50 Common Signs and Symptoms of Stress," The American Institute of Stress, accessed January 27, 2021.

45 "Wayfinder Life Coach Training," Martha Beck, accessed January 27, 2021.

46 Julia Cameron, *The Artist's Way* (New York: TarcherPerigee, 2016).

47 "Video: Breathing Exercises: 4-7-8 Breath," Andrew Weil, M.D., accessed January 27, 2021.

48 "Giving thanks can make you happier," Harvard Health Publishing, November 2011.

49 Jim Robbins, "Ecopsychology: How Immersion in Nature Benefits Your Health," Yale Environment 360, January 9, 2020.

50 Ibid.

51 Carla, Lind, *The Wright Style: Re-Creating the Spirit of Frank Lloyd Wright* (New York: Simon & Schuster, 1992).

52 Magdalena Van den Berg, et al., "Autonomic Nervous System Responses to Viewing Green and Built Settings: Differentiating Between Sympathetic and Parasympathetic Activity," *International Journal of Environmental Research and Public Health* 12, no. 12, 2015.

53 Gustavo Razetti, "The Ego Is Not the Enemy," Fearless Culture, December 23, 2018.

54 Doris Jeanette, "Ego or Authentic Self?" Trans4mind, accessed January 28, 2021.

55 Sangharakshita, *The Taste of Freedom: Approaches to the Buddhist Path.* Cambridge (UK: Wildhorse Publications, 1997).

56 Jakob Nielsen and Jen Cardello, "The Halo Effect," Nielsen Norman Group, November 9, 2013.

57 "The Work Is a Practice," The Work of Byron Katie, accessed January 28, 2021.

58 Mateo Sol, "5 Ways to Develop Self-Worth (When You Never Feel Good Enough)," LonerWolf.

59 "Qi (Chi): The Taoist Principle of Life Force," Learn Religions, June 25, 2019.

60 "Prana," Merriam-Webster (Merriam-Webster), accessed January 31, 2021, https://www.merriam-webster.com/dictionary/prana.

61 J Zhao and Xiao-xu Li, "An Approach to the nature of Qi in TCM-Qi and Bioenergy," 2012.

62 "The Chi and the Yin and Yang," Feng Shui Natural, accessed January 31, 2021.

63 "Yin and Yang Theory," Traditional Chinese Medicine World Foundation, accessed January 31, 2021.

64 "Form vs. Matter," Stanford Encyclopedia of Philosophy, updated March 25, 2020.

65 Hans Andeweg, "Everything is Energy, Everything is One, Everything is Possible," Turner Publishing, April 21, 2016.

66 Debra Rose Wilson, "11 Benefits of Burning Sage, How to Get Started, and More," Healthline, updated June 22, 2020.

67 Dhwty, "The Ancient Art of Smudging: From Banishing Evil to Curing Ailments," Ancient Origins, updated November 11, 2018.

68 Kristen Nunez, "What Is Palo Santo, and How Is It Used Medicinally?" Healthline, August 11, 2020.

69 Bess O'Connor, "Clear Your Energy and Lift Your Spirits With the Sacred Art of Smudging," Chopra, Agust 14, 2019.

70 Joanie Yanusas, "3 Essential Oils to Help You Set Boundaries," accessed January 31, 2021.

71 "The History of Aromatherapy Pt 1: 3,500 BC- 199 AD," Quintessence Aromatherapy, accessed January 31, 2021.

72 Brent A. Bauer, "What are the benefits of aromatherapy?" Mayo Clinic, June 6, 2020.

73 "What Do Negative Ions Do?" Course Hero, accessed January 31, 2021.

74 Della Bobian, "Essential Oils and Non-Toxic Cleaning Around the House," accessed January 31, 2021.

75 "Bleeding and Diluting Essential Oils," Aura Cacia, accessed January 31, 2021.

76 "Crystal," Merriam-Webster (Merriam-Webster), accessed January 31, 2021, https://www.merriam-webster.com/dictionary/crystal.

77 Terah Kathryn Collins, The Three Sisters of the Tao (Carlsbad, CA: Hay House, 2010).

78 "Feng shui," Merriam-Webster (Merriam-Webster), accessed January 31, 2021, https://www.merriam-webster.com/dictionary/feng%20shui.

79 "About Feng Shui," Black Sect Esoteric Buddhism: Yun Lin Temple, accessed January 31, 2021.

80 "About Feng Shui," BTB Feng Shui School, accessed January 31, 2021.

81 Victor Kim, "The Five Elements in Taoism and Eastern Medicine," Tao Universe, November 26, 2018.

82   Anne Batty, "Feng Shui – Earth Wisdom Practice," *San Clemente Journal,* May 1, 2001.

83   "Balancing Feng Shui's Five Elements, Part 1: The Creative Cycle," Open Spaces Feng Shui, accessed February 1, 2021.

84   Ibid.

85   "5 Elements," The Fengshui Academy, accessed February 1, 2021.

86   Rodika Tchi, "The Feng Shui 5 Elements Theory of Cycles," August 4, 2019.

87   Laura Cerrano, "Feng Shui Bagua Map Basics For Your Home in 4 Easy Steps," *Feng Shui Manhattan,* June 27, 2020.

88   Kendra Cherry, "Color Psychology: Does It Affect How You Feel?" *Verywellmind,* updated May 28, 2020.

89   Anita Naik, "Natural light vs artificial light: what are the effects on our health?" *Netdoctor,* May 20, 2020.

90   Summer Allen, "The Science of Gratitude," Greater Good Science Center, May 2018.

91   "Circadian Rhythms," National Institute of General Medical Sciences, accessed February 1, 2021.

92   Stephen Westland, "Here's How Colours Really Affect Our Brain And Body, According to Science," *Science Alert,* September 30, 2017.

93   "The Color of the Light Affects the Circadian Rhythms," Centers for Disease Control and Prevention, updated April 1, 2020.

94   Ben P. Stein "Do White LEDs Disrupt our Biological Clocks?" *Inside Science,* October 14, 2011.

95   Nicole Martins Ferreira, "Color Psychology: How Color Meanings Affect Your Brand," *Oberlo,* May 31, 2019.

96   "The Science of Color," Smithsonian Libraries, accessed February 1, 2021.

97   Ibid.

98   Huiran Zhang and Zheng Tang, "To judge what color the subject watched by color effect on brain activity," *International Journal of Computer Science and Network Security* 11, no. 2, 2011.

99   "What was It with Picasso and Blue?" Phaidon, accessed February 1, 2021.

100 "What is True Colors?" *True Colors,* accessed February 1, 2021.

101 "What's Your Personality Color?" *Psychologia,* accessed February 1, 2021.

102 Domicele Jonauskaite, et al., "Pink for Girls, Red for Boys, and Blue for Both Genders: Colour Preferences in Children and Adults," *Sex Roles* 80, August 27, 2018.

103 "Color Psychology," *Color Psychology,* accessed February 1, 2021.

104 "Sour mood getting you down? Get back to nature," Harvard Health Publishing, July 2018.

105 Carla Lind, *The Wright Style* (New York: Simon & Schuster, 1992).

106   Richard Neutra, *Survival Through Design*. (Oxford, UK: Oxford University Press, 1954).

107   Maarten Overdijk, "Richard Neutra's Therapeutic Architecture," *Failed Architecture*, November 2, 2015.

108   Van den Berg, et al., "Autonomic Nervous System Responses to Viewing Green and Built Settings."

109   Emily Vidovich, "Bringing the Outdoors In: The Benefits of Biophilia," NRDC, June 23, 2020.

110   Margaret E. Sears and Stephen J. Genuis, "Environmental Determinants of Chronic Disease and Medical Approaches: Recognition, Avoidance, Supportive Therapy, and Detoxification," *Journal of Environmental and Public Health*, 2012.

111   Dianne Price, "Researchers look to toxins in the environment for answers to Alzheimer's," Arizona State University, November 26, 2019.

112   Rosemarie G. Ramos and Kenneth Olden, "Gene-Environment Interactions in the Development of Complex Disease Phenotypes," *International Journal of Environmental Research and Public Health* 5, no. 1, 2008.

113   "Volatile Organic Compounds' Impact on Indoor Air Quality," United States Environmental Protection Agency, accessed February 2, 2021.

114   Monica Amarelo, "EWG Lists the Top 10 Toxic Chemicals EPA Should Review Now," EWG, July 21, 2016.

115   "Healthy people in healthy places equals a healthy economy," USGBC, accessed February 2, 2021.

116   "Electromagnetic hypersensitivity," Australia Radiation Protection and Nuclear Safety Agency, accessed February 2, 2021.

117   "5 Benefits of Houseplants," *Bioadvanced*, accessed February 2, 2021.

118   B.C. Wolverton, et al., "Interior Landscape Plants for Indoor Air Pollution," NASA, September 5, 1989.

119   Ibid.

120   Ibid.

121   Robert Hutchins, "8 Surprising Health Benefits of Gardening," UNC Health Talk, May 18, 2020.

122   Penelope Hobhouse, "Beth Chatto obituary," *The Guardian*, May 14, 2018.

123   "Reducing and Reusing Basics," United States Environmental Protection Agency, accessed February 2, 2021.

124   Mike Oppland, "8 Ways To Creare Flow According to Mihaly Csikszentmihalyi," *Positive Psychology*, December 10, 2020.

125   John J. Pitney, "Honest, Mr. President: Abe Never Said It," NPR, March 25, 2010.

ACKNOWLEDGMENTS

WRITING A BOOK IS A SOLITARY JOURNEY BUT publishing it takes a village. I want to thank everyone at Book Launchers that helped me make *Om for the hOMe* a reality. Your guidance and patience with me during this process was greatly appreciated. Genie Davis you are a rock star editor. Clodagh, you enhanced my life with your act of kindness and generosity.

I am grateful for clients that entrusted me to help them Live BeautiFULLY. As I taught you, you taught me. The lens with which I experienced this journey unfold became clearer and clearer because of your willingness to be vulnerable and go where the work took us.

A special acknowledgment to M.B. You were very much a part of this journey. I am most proud that we showed the boys the road less traveled was the high road, and family is defined in many ways. Rachel and Matthew, love is love is love. Susan, you lift me up when I fall down and are always there when I need you. That is the greatest gift – of one's self.

CPSIA information can be obtained
at www.ICGtesting.com
Printed in the USA
BVHW090058190921
616980BV00004B/11